"In this elegantly written and engaging book [...] us with a kind of biography of the book of R[...] content, ancestors, and original context, thro[...] some of its later illuminated manuscripts) and onto its contemporary message in an age of environmental crisis. Kiel not only provides an accessible introduction to Revelation but also powerfully makes the case that John's critique of the ecological destructiveness of the Roman Empire can challenge us today—and can inform and shape a scientifically informed but radical response to the economic and environmental problems we face. The rich combination of historical contextualization, careful and critical interpretation, and informed contemporary reflection make this book an ideal stimulus to fresh thought, both about the book of Revelation (and Christian eschatology more generally) and about our contemporary environmental crisis."

> —David G. Horrell
> Professor of New Testament Studies
> University of Exeter, UK

"For many, the book of Revelation is self-evidently detrimental to environmental concerns. In this engaging and provocative book, full of rich insights on every page, Micah Kiel forces readers to think again. Once we allow that Revelation's terrifying vision of environmental catastrophe is more descriptive than prescriptive, an ancient visionary response to deforestation and water and air pollution, new possibilities open up for us. Kiel skillfully uncovers dimensions of Revelation that reveal humanity's connectedness to the earth, to animal and vegetable life, dimensions acknowledged by many of the book's medieval illuminators. He challenges us to swallow our anthropocentric pride and enter into its vision in which nonhuman animals lead the way to a proper orientation of the cosmos. Most important, he unleashes Revelation's surprisingly rich potential for developing a contemporary, theocentric ecology."

> —Ian Boxall
> Associate Professor of New Testament
> The Catholic University of America

"In his innovative study of Revelation, Micah D. Kiel employs different strategies to show what Revelation's 'apocalyptic ecology' can offer the environmental crisis. His most challenging question concerns the book's depiction of earth's destruction. How can a book where the sea is annihilated contribute positively to ecological consciousness? In the refusal of John of Patmos to diminish his critique of the Roman Empire, and it's devastating effect on the earth, lies Revelation's theocentric vision of nothing less than a new earth.

"Revelation is not an anthropocentric book. The earth protects the woman from the dragon, and birds refuse to let evil have the last word. But humankind is not passive in the drama of John's eschatology. In his engaging eco-critical journey through the historical contexts that have formed John's theology to the illuminated manuscripts that depict Revelation's legacy, Kiel shows that Revelation's apocalyptic eschatology provides a robust call to ecological action. Biblical students and scholars alike will find in *Apocalyptic Ecology* much inspiration for ecological hope."

— Marie Turner
Flinders University of South Australia

Apocalyptic Ecology

The Book of Revelation, the Earth, and the Future

Micah D. Kiel

Foreword by
Barbara R. Rossing

A Michael Glazier Book

LITURGICAL PRESS
Collegeville, Minnesota

www.litpress.org

A Michael Glazier Book published by Liturgical Press

1   2   3   4   5   6   7   8   9

Library of Congress Cataloging-in-Publication Data

Names: Kiel, Micah D., author.
Title: Apocalyptic ecology : the book of Revelation, the earth, and the future / Micah D. Kiel.
Description: Collegeville, Minnesota : Liturgical Press, 2017. | Includes bibliographical references and index. | Description based on print version record and CIP data provided by publisher; resource not viewed.
Identifiers: LCCN 2017005968 (print) | LCCN 2017029827 (ebook) | ISBN 9780814687833 (ebook) | ISBN 9780814687826
Subjects: LCSH: Bible. Revelation—Criticism, interpretation, etc. | Earth (Planet)—Forecasting.
Classification: LCC BS646 (ebook) | LCC BS646 .K54 2017 (print) | DDC 228/.06—dc23
LC record available at https://lccn.loc.gov/2017005968

For my sons, Harrison and Brendan:
May Psalm 148 always ground your worldview

Contents

Foreword

Barbara R. Rossing

Our planet is in trouble. As fears of the "end" convulse our culture, the biblical book of Revelation can help us hear Earth's urgent pleas on behalf of the whole creation. Micah Kiel's *Apocalyptic Ecology* makes an exciting contribution to the study of the Apocalypse within the emerging scholarly discipline of ecological hermeneutics. This book diagnoses our current ecological crisis in light of Revelation's critique of the way the ancient Roman Empire abused the natural world. Most important, it shows us hope for our future.

Three elements make *Apocalyptic Ecology* especially important. First, the attention to art: Kiel introduces us to the exuberant and colorful world of illuminated illustrations of Revelation by medieval and Gothic artists. He shows us their love of nature. It turns out that in the early Middle Ages people's attention was captured not by the toxic aspects of Revelation but by the book's rich zoological life, the saving grace of birds and animals praising God. The Trier Manuscript gives us Earth as a fully personified figure opening her mouth to save the heavenly woman and her child. The Beatus Manuscript adds a Noah's ark interlude, transporting the living world of Noah's animals into the Apocalypse—animals of every color look out at us from the windows of the boat. These medieval artists paint Revelation as a book of joy and vibrant hope for life. Their "visual exegesis" of Revelation shows us God's beloved world, including animals, our kin.

Second, the structure of *Apocalyptic Ecology* takes us on a journey over time, interpreting Revelation's environmental consciousness over multiple generations. We are introduced to Revelation's "ancestry" in the Jewish apocalyptic tradition of resistance to empires, and to Revelation's later career and legacy. Not every scholar can make the apocryphal book of *1 Enoch* interesting, but Kiel does so— and wonderfully. Revelation draws on *1 Enoch*, a book infused with creation imagery to critique the brutalities of Hellenistic conquests. *Apocalyptic Ecology* reveals the environmental impacts of warfare: the devastation of animals, forests, and agriculture. It also deconstructs the underlying logic of military ideology, using archaeological and textual evidence from inscriptions and coins. This book makes a contribution to empire-critical scholarship as well as to ecological hermeneutics.

Revelation engages in a battle of imaginations over who controls the universe. This is the third and most important contribution. The chapters on Revelation in the context in the Roman Empire—what Kiel calls Revelation's "Upbringing"—bring impressive new details and insights about the Roman Empire's totalizing claims of empire. Revelation "fights back" against imperial systems of cruelty and conquest, against an economy fueled by destructive mining, deforestation, trade, and slaughter of animals. In Kiel's most original contribution, he introduces us to the *venationes*, the mind-bending killing of animals for entertainment in public spectacles. The massive slaughter in the arenas of cities throughout the Mediterranean actually drove species to the brink of extinction. Kiel suggests that one reason Revelation opposes eating meat offered to idols is that the meat may have been that of animals killed in such gruesome spectacles. Domination of the animal kingdom constitutes an obscene affront to the role of God as creator. Revelation exposes and critiques such domination as idolatry.

Revelation's "personality" can be a challenge for the biographer. Yet Kiel's novel biographical approach is compelling reading. Some of his best writing comes when he relates Revelation to popular culture, including films and poetry. The question of annihilation or renewal—the degree to which Revelation insists that our Earth must be destroyed—finds no easy resolution. Kiel is a gentle and fascinating guide, helping us grapple with today's urgent questions.

Preface

The world is too much with us; late and soon,
Getting and spending, we lay waste our powers;
Little we see in Nature that is ours;
We have given our hearts away, a sordid boon!
This Sea that bares her bosom to the moon;
The winds that will be howling at all hours,
And are up-gathered now like sleeping flowers;
For this, for everything, we are out of tune;
It moves us not. Great God! I'd rather be
A Pagan suckled in a creed outworn;
So might I, standing on this pleasant lea,
Have glimpses that would make me less forlorn;
Have sight of Proteus rising from the sea;
Or hear old Triton blow his wreathèd horn.

—William Wordsworth

The Wordsworth poem above laments a relationship between humanity and nature that has gone awry. He longs for another worldview and creed through which he can experience the natural world with awe and wonder. In this book, I will argue that the book of Revelation provides such a worldview. The book of Revelation envisions an entirely new reality, which is exactly what we need in order to survive our modern ecological crisis and to overcome the malaise we feel when thinking about the future. Revelation's "Apocalyptic Ecology" challenges the foundations of a society that destroys the earth and rarely has to face the consequences; its suggestions are radical and dangerous. Writing this book has changed me. I hope that understanding Revelation's message, and thinking about it in light of modern ecology, will have a similar impact on my readers.

Most of the work on this book was completed in conjunction with a sabbatical leave granted to me in the fall of 2015 by St. Ambrose University. I am grateful to the administration at St. Ambrose for granting this sabbatical, and to my colleagues in the Theology Department for supporting it unfailingly. Lisa Powell took over for me as department chair during my absence, for which the words "Thank you" hardly suffice. Upon my return, the St. Ambrose library staff, particularly the interlibrary loan office, have helped me immensely. I also received help from stalwart work study students: Madison Schramer, Lauren Schroeder, Autum Yarger, and Delina Tesfamichael.

I spent my sabbatical as a resident scholar at the Collegeville Institute for Ecumenical and Cultural Research in Collegeville, MN. My family packed up in August, my wife took a leave of absence from her job (thanks, Fr. Jim Vrba), my kids changed schools, and we moved to the shores of Stumpf Lake for the semester. The institute's staff, Carla and Jan, made us feel at home. Don Ottenhoff was a great resource and leads an amazing program. My family and I were enriched by the community of scholars, leaders, and pastors at the Collegeville Institute. I would like to thank Richard Gaillardetz in particular for his friendship, exemplified in walking to noon prayer together, chats over baseball, racquetball games, and listening to tales of my fishing exploits.

The monastic community warmly welcomed our family as well. We extend our gratitude to Fr. Bob Koopmann, Fr. Timothy Backous, Br. Paul Richards, Fr. Anthony Ruff, and Sr. Colman O'Connell, among many others, for their friendship and camaraderie during our time there. The liturgical life and the natural setting at Saint John's were a constant source of peace, beauty, and inspiration during our stay. The services offered to me through Alcuin Library were efficient and professional, making my work possible. I also would like to thank Fr. Columba Stewart and Matthew Heinzelmann for their hospitality at the Hill Monastic Manuscript Library, whose resources I utilized for the research in chapter four of this book. I also benefited from conversations with Fr. Michael Patella and Charles Bobertz, both of the Saint John's School of Theology. Tim Ternes was kind enough to give me a private tour of the Saint John's Bible originals, a very moving experience. I am deeply grateful to all of the great people at Liturgical Press. Peter and Hans met with me early in the writing process, which was very helpful. All of the staff, Tara, Colleen, and Lauren, were prompt in answering my many questions and consistently professional and encouraging.

Our Collegeville experience would have failed miserably had our children not been well cared for. Cheri Burg and Betty Pundsack, who taught our kids at All Saint's Academy in St. Joseph, were gracious and caring, knowing that our children would be there only for a semester. We also had a lot of fun with Allison and Carl Driggins and family, who lived on the other side of Fruit Farm Road and hosted us more times than I can count.

Shortly after returning from sabbatical, I was diagnosed with a rare benign tumor called Vestibular Schwannoma. These tumors grow on the eighth cranial nerve that connects the ear with the brain. In May 2016 I had major skull-base surgery to remove the tumor. I express my gratitude to Dr. Marlan Hansen and his team of doctors and nurses at the University of Iowa Hospital. They helped me avoid serious complications from this condition and treatment. Had the outcome been different, it certainly would have jeopardized my ability to complete this book.

This book was also made possible by the incredible work of the many scholars and teachers who have gone before me. Much of this will be documented in the footnotes and bibliography. There have been many foundational treatments of the book of Revelation from which I have benefited. At the same time, recent treatments of the Bible and ecology have set new and interesting directions for my field. Specifically, I am grateful to my colleague Robert Grant and my friend Peter Lane, both of whom read and commented on an early draft. Barbara Rossing graciously read and commented on the full manuscript. She offered many important insights and saved me from some potentially embarrassing mistakes. Despite this help, any remaining errors are, to quote Blind Willie Johnson, "nobody's fault but mine."

Finally, to my family, I offer my fullest gratitude. They tackled the sabbatical challenge with aplomb. My wife, Eleanor, read several iterations of the manuscript and has, as always, been an insightful first reader. She also has listened to me talk things through over countless walks, drives, or martinis. It is to my boys, Harrison and Brendan, that I dedicate this book. They are a constant source of joy, wonder, and love. I am hopeful for the future world they will inhabit.

Micah D. Kiel
Davenport, IA
4 October 2016
Memorial of St. Francis of Assisi

Acknowledgments

Image of Claudius from Aphrodisias used by permission of Roger B. Ulrich.

Image of Gladiator from Nenning used by permission of Carole Raddato (from her blog, followinghadrian.com).

Images from Trinity Apocalypse provided by Master and Fellows of Trinity College Cambridge. Thanks also to Sandy Paul.

Adaptation of map of Roman Asia by permission from Accordance by Oak Tree Software.

Images of the Morgan Beatus, MS M.644, folios 79r, 109r, 174v, 215v, 220r, 223r, purchased by J. P. Morgan (1867–1943) in 1919. Used by permission of the Pierpont Morgan Library, New York, NY.

Image of Trier Apocalypse by permission of Stadtbibliothek/Stadtarchiv Trier, Germany. Thanks also to Anja Runkel.

Images of the *Saint John's Bible* by permission. Thanks also to Tim Ternes.

Introduction

Burnmarks and Biography: Guiding Metaphors

"Revelation takes us on a journey . . . into the heart of God, a journey into the heart of our world."[1]

—Barbara Rossing

I. The Bible's Environmental Legacy: A Sharp Two-edged Sword

The movie theater darkens. (Most) people silence their cell phones. The extensive previews end and the movie begins. The film slaps its watchers with raging seas, scorched earth, and meteors falling from the sky. People run. Cities are consumed. The end is nigh.

A preoccupation with "the end" is in our DNA. We could not escape it even if we tried. The apocalypse offers us a libretto that reveals how things will play out. The apocalypse often lies dormant, but it will surface at any natural disaster, terrorist attack, rare lunar eclipse, or five-hundred-year-old Mayan calendar. As Robert Frost

---

1. Barbara R. Rossing, *The Rapture Exposed: The Message of Hope in the Book of Revelation* (New York: Basic Books, 2004), xviii.

famously put it: "Some say the world will end in fire, some say in ice."[2] In either case, the world *will* end and we are preoccupied with the manner of that end.

The manner of "the end" has become explicitly environmental in recent decades. Scientific descriptions of environmental degradation suggest that we might be the cause of our own undoing. We hear predictions on a weekly basis about the dangers of deforestation, loss of biodiversity, and rising global temperatures. The sea could inundate New York City in fifty to eighty years.[3] The decline in bees and their ability to pollinate threatens crop production, food security, and human well-being.[4] In all likelihood we now are in the midst of the sixth great extinction in the history of our planet.[5] There is no scientific doubt: we face an environmental crisis.

Although our crisis has us thinking about the end, it also ought to get us thinking about the beginning. Our environmental crisis is not just a modern problem. It is a human problem. Humans have been having a negative ecological impact since our culture emerged. Thus, it is a cultural problem. We have embedded in our culture certain traditions that justify our exploitation and destruction of the environment. In a widely cited article from 1967, Lynn White lays responsibility for the environmental crisis at the feet of the Christian tradition. White's arguments form the starting point for virtually every theological book on the environment because he states the problem simply and clearly: humans, he says, are "conditioned by beliefs about our nature and destiny—that is, by religion." He goes on to say: "More science and more technology are not going to get us out of the present ecologic crisis until we find a new religion, or rethink our old one."[6]

2. Edward Connery Lathem, *The Poetry of Robert Frost* (New York: Holt and Company, 1969), 220.

3. Vivien Gornitz, Stephen Couch, and Ellen Hartig, "Impacts of Sea Level Rise in the New York City Metropolitan Area," *Global and Planetary Change* 32 (2001): 61–88.

4. Simon Potts et al., "Global Pollinator Declines: Trends, Impacts and Drivers," *Trends in Ecology and Evolution* 25 (2010): 345–53.

5. S. L. Pimm et al., "The Biodiversity of Species and Their Rates of Extinction, Distribution, and Protection," *Science* 344 (2014): 1246752-1–1246752-10.

6. Lynn White Jr., "The Historical Roots of our Ecologic Crisis," *Science* 155 (1967): 1205–6.

The Bible is the primary virus in Lynn White's diagnosis. Its legacy on environmental concerns is, to borrow a biblical image, a sharp two-edged sword. On one hand, the dominion given to humanity over creation in the book of Genesis has long been detrimental to the earth. In the book of Genesis, the first creation myth culminates in the creation of humanity. God immediately sets them over the other things that have been created:

> and let them have dominion over the fish of the sea, and over the birds of the air, and over the cattle, and over all the wild animals of the earth, and over every creeping thing that creeps upon the earth. (Gen 1:26)

Two verses later, after creating male and female in the divine image, God reiterates and expands upon their role:

> God blessed them, and God said to them, "Be fruitful and multiply, and fill the earth and subdue it; and have dominion over the fish of the sea and over the birds of the air and over every living thing that moves upon the earth." (Gen 1:28)

We have interpreted these verses to give us carte blanche to do whatever we want to the world around us.[7]

On the other hand, the Bible contains beautiful and passionate language about the necessity and importance of creation, its integral role in understanding God, and its merit and beauty irrespective of humanity. The creation myth in Genesis 1 deems creation "good" long before humanity arrives on the stage. The Psalms are a treasure of poetry about the importance of God and creation:

> He covers the heavens with clouds,
>   prepares rain for the earth,
>   makes grass grow on the hills.
> He gives to the animals their food,
>   and to the young ravens when they cry. (Ps 147:8-9)

---

7. For a historical overview of this text's influence, see chapter 2, "Dominion Interpreted—A Historical Account," in Richard Bauckham, *Living with Other Creatures: Green Exegesis and Theology* (Waco, TX: Baylor University Press, 2011), 14–62.

Psalm 148 describes all the things of creation praising God:

> Praise the LORD from the earth,
>   you sea monsters and all deeps,
> fire and hail, snow and frost,
>   stormy wind fulfilling his command!
> Mountains and all hills,
>   fruit trees and all cedars!
> Wild animals and all cattle,
>   creeping things and flying birds! (Ps 148:7-10)

The final chapters of the book of Job offer a vision of creation devoid of humanity altogether, undoing the anthropocentrism in Genesis chapter 1. In the New Testament, Jesus's exhortation to consider the ravens and the lilies (for example, Luke 12:22-31), which are beautiful and thrive because of God's creative providence, reiterates the same idea of the goodness of creation and its internal harmony.

Despite these positive strains, lauded by figures like Francis of Assisi, the Bible's environmental legacy is often perceived as overwhelmingly negative. In the beginning we started destroying because the Bible's beginning told us we should.

II. The Bible and the Apocalypse: "Biblical Burnmarks"

If the Bible's myths of the beginning establish an environmentally problematic precedent, its visions of the end offer little reprieve. Many biblical texts—some of the prophets, portions of the gospels, and Revelation—present a scenario in which the earth must endure a series of upheavals before the end of time. Jesus in the Gospel of Mark describes an end of the ages that includes earthquakes and famines (Mark 13:8). Ultimately, "in those days, after that suffering, the sun will be darkened, and the moon will not give its light, and the stars will be falling from heaven, and the powers in the heavens will be shaken" (13:24-25). These words of cosmic upheaval are reminiscent of a variety of texts from the Hebrew Bible, including the prophets Isaiah, Joel, and Ezekiel. The book of Revelation is even more explicit. It suggests that God will create a new heaven and a new earth, because "the first earth had passed away, and the sea was no more" (Rev 21:1). These future-oriented texts suggest that at the time before the end, the fabric of creation itself will be ripped apart. Such a view of the future offers no reason for humans to nurture nature.

The Bible's eschatology continues to be intricately entwined with our environmental outlook today. On Twitter, a prominent Christian leader is reported to have said: "I know who created the earth and he is coming back to burn it up. So yeah, I drive an SUV." Such a brash statement allows us to see the "biblical burnmarks" in today's society.[8] In a text like the book of Revelation, the ecosphere seems to be left smoldering, degraded, or completely destroyed. In the future God will create a new heaven and a new earth, which obviates the need for care of the environment. We must grapple with the fact that the eschatology (the view of the end) in apocalyptic literature might be at odds with a properly scientific environmental ethic.

If we recognize this problem, perhaps we should just get rid of it. Let's stop reading Revelation, find something to replace it, and hope for a better outcome. This, however, may not be possible. The problem with dismissing the ancient world's apocalyptic literature is that, as our movie theaters tell us, we are an apocalyptic people. We must acknowledge the "tenacity, the width, and the versatility" of the apocalypse in our culture.[9] It "metabolizes" both inside and outside ourselves.[10] We cannot escape it, even if we wanted to.

Nor should we escape it. Revelation is Scripture, and as such, needs a constant engagement. We return, then, to the challenge from Lynn White. Rather than jettison, we must reexamine and rethink those traditions that have formed us. My contention in this book is that ancient apocalyptic literature, and the book of Revelation in particular, is not detrimental to environmental concerns. On the contrary, this literature offers a rich environmental point of view, if properly understood. In the chapters that follow I will employ several different strategies in order properly to understand the book of Revelation and what an "apocalyptic ecology" can offer to our modern environmental crisis.

8. Catherine Keller, *Apocalypse Now and Then: A Feminist Guide to the End of the World* (Boston: Beacon Press, 1996), 20.

9. Ibid., 9.

10. Ibid., xii.

The phrase "apocalyptic ecology" is a bit of an oxymoron. Strictly speaking, ecology is a branch of the biological sciences that studies ecosystems and the relationship among organisms and their surroundings. "Environmentalism" is a term and field more suited to the humanities. I will attempt to limit use of the word "ecology" to its scientific sense. I will make an exception, however, for this book's title and guiding metaphor. When I use the phrase "apocalyptic ecology" I do not mean to imply that there is a scientific view that can or will emerge from the book of Revelation. The book of Revelation comes to us, however, because of a series of relationships it has had with its surroundings, many of which we will explore in the pages of this book. Ultimately, I hope this book will offer a constructive proposal for how Revelation can contribute positively to our modern concern about care for the environment. The word "ecology" comes from a Greek word that refers to a house or dwelling place, and, by extension, can refer to the family that dwells there. An apocalyptic ecology will be an exploration of Revelation's potential role in and interaction with the planet and its inhabitants.

III. Revelation's Biography: A Guiding Metaphor

Imagine that you are writing a biography of a famous person. How might you structure such an endeavor? What components would it have? A biography would trace a person's ancestry. A biography might explore the world and situation in which a person was raised—her or his upbringing. We might ask about a person's personality: what was she or he like? Any biography would discuss a person's career: what did this person do and why was it significant? Finally, a biography ought to consider a person's legacy. How will she or he be remembered? Biography is always interpretive. Steve Jobs, the founder of Apple computers, died in 2011 but nobody can agree on how to interpret his life. We know most of what he said and did, but biographers and film directors do not agree on basic components of his legacy: which elements are truly constitutive of his mark on society? How ought his life to be interpreted?

Thinking about a biography will help us understand the book of Revelation and its ecological contribution. Although obviously not a person, Revelation has all the same components we might look for in a person's biography:

Personality: Franklin D. Roosevelt's personality was a key component of his presidency. He was known for his overwhelmingly positive attitude. How did the way he presented himself influence his work and life? The process of examining how Revelation presents itself, what it says and what it is made of, is called "exegesis." This entails letting a text's meaning emerge from the details of what it says, to "read out" its meaning. Although Revelation's depiction of the environment seems overwhelmingly negative at first, does such a view hold up to scrutiny? What are the text's main features? Its habits? Have we understood its symbolism properly? How do individual episodes coordinate with the whole? What ecological conclusions emerge from a close reading of this text's personality?

Ancestors: Leopold Mozart's role in the movie *Amadeus* demonstrates the importance of ancestors. By the end of Mozart's life (and the movie) the father's overbearing nature haunts the son, explaining how Mozart's life unfolded. Ancestors influence biblical texts as well. Revelation is infused with inherited texts, traditions, practices, and beliefs. Many ancient Jews and Christians were fond of apocalyptic literature. It is not always possible to draw direct lines of contact between this antecedent literature and Revelation, but an in-depth exploration of some of the predecessors—the extant motifs, emphases, and catalysts—will illuminate that which Revelation inherited.

Upbringing: Rosa Parks exemplifies the importance of context, in her case, unjust segregation, in forging someone's identity and actions. The Bible does not fall into our laps straight from the lips of God. Human beings wrote the Bible in specific situations and for specific reasons. Revelation is shaped by its context, written during the Roman Empire. The book results from the union of a community and a context. Exploring the ideological, theological, and natural environments in which Revelation was raised will allow us to contextualize its view of creation and the natural world.

Career: The career of Dorothy Day resulted in the Catholic Worker movement. She exerted influence and created change. A biography ought to consider a person's career. What has Revelation done? Who read it and what impact did it have? Has Revelation had a negative impact on the ecological imaginations of communities across the centuries? What are its skills, its competencies, its "growth areas"?

Legacy: Legacies are tricky. For instance, what is the legacy of Christopher Columbus? Long considered a hero, he now is increasingly understood as an antagonist. Legacies are determined and shaped; they are not self-evident. Once we know what Revelation has done, how do we assess its legacy? Are there reasons to sweep it into the dustbin of history? Is its ecological legacy mostly negative? Or are there ways to harness its power for a new age? Is there an apocalyptic ecology for our world today?

The concept of a biography, applied to a text almost two thousand years old, will allow us to look at Revelation from a variety of points of view. Like a doctor practicing holistic medicine, here we will look at Revelation's "whole person." This will give us as complete a picture as possible of Revelation's past, present, and future role in environmental discussion, with all its warts and beauty on display.

IV. Preview

Science alone cannot convince people that care for the earth is important. A recent study concluded that "a communication strategy that focuses only on transmission of sound scientific information" is unlikely ultimately to be effective so long as the "debate continues to feature cultural meanings that divide citizens of opposing worldviews."[11] Data and facts will not persuade people to change the way they live. Faith, however, shapes people's moral actions—or

11. Dan M. Kahan et al., "The Polarizing Impact of Science Literacy and Numeracy on Perceived Climate Change Risks," *Nature Climate Change* 2, no. 10 (2012): 8–9.

at least it purports to. While the book of Revelation may not be the first place one might think of looking for environmentally helpful moral guidance, by the end of this book I hope to show that this indeed can be the case. I offer here a brief preview of the conclusion each chapter will reach.

In chapter one (Revelation's personality), we begin getting to know Revelation itself: who wrote it, when and where was it written, and what strategies are necessary for its interpretation. Then we turn and have a deeper conversation about its view of the future. Deciding whether John envisions continuity between our world and God's future creation will figure prominently in how we read the book's environmental contribution (or lack thereof). What we find in Revelation's ecological personality is hope, something that is increasingly difficult to find in environmental discussions in our world today.

In chapter two (Revelation's ancestors) we look backward to a time before the book of Revelation. We will meet a Jewish community who interpreted the world around them in apocalyptic ways and wrote about it in apocalyptic language, forms, and motifs. This literature, like Revelation, describes a world left smoldering in the ruins of apocalyptic warfare. They did this, however, not because they thought God wanted to destroy the world, but as a way of expressing dismay over the suffering and destruction they themselves were experiencing. What the authors of these texts offer is an environmental alternative. They envision a reality that bears little resemblance to the one created by humans.

In chapter three (Revelation's upbringing) we will discuss the world in which John formed his opinions. This world was ruled by Rome and its economic, religious, and political agenda and propaganda. These things were opposed to John's belief in God and way of existence modeled by Jesus. Revelation offers a profound critique of empire. Part of that critique extends even to environmental devastation. Any capitulation with the economic agenda of an empire means one will have the wrong allegiance. The cosmos does not belong to Rome but to God, and an apocalyptic ecology based on the book of Revelation will use this as the starting point for moral action in the environmental realm.

Chapter four (Revelation's career) moves forward through time to discuss how the book of Revelation has been read across the

xxvi   *Apocalyptic Ecology*

centuries. Because it is such a vivid book, it has spawned many wild interpretations throughout Christian history. Since the ecosphere plays such a vital role in Revelation, it is worth asking how Revelation has shaped the ecological imagination of its readers. Does it tend to lead to destruction and violence against creation? In the examples I have selected—limited here to illuminated manuscripts—Revelation does not seem to prod violence against nature. Instead, it calls its readers and viewers into contemplation of the way God, humans, and the environment are all connected.

In chapter five (Revelation's legacy) we will discern what emerges from Revelation in forming an environmental ethic. While the author of Revelation was not an environmental activist, his work does provide certain insights into the future, empire, and economic lust, categories that prove operative in our world today. Although John's apocalypse is about the end, what it really calls for is a new beginning. Given our current perilous ecological situation, a new beginning is exactly what we need.

Albert Einstein is often quoted as saying, "The significant problems we face today cannot be solved at the same level of thinking we were at when we created them." Almost all of our ways of trying to solve the ecological crisis emerge from the same system of thinking that caused the problem in the first place: a trust in technology, an anthropocentric worldview, and individualistic initiatives. We live embedded in a culture that makes it very difficult for us to have perspective on the root causes of our environmental crisis. We engage unthinkingly in habitual behavior with no regard for its environmental impact. Even if it is not our fault, we can still be guilty. John Ehrenfeld explains how our cultural situation occludes our vision by using the image of fish that swim in an ocean:

> Given our total immersion in this culture, extraordinary steps are required even to recognize this form of habitual behavior, much less begin to try and change it. After all, that is what culture is: the ocean we all swim in and cannot sense ordinarily. Unlike fish, however, we can become conscious of the deep structures that drive our routines by stepping outside them and, with considerable effort, change them. If we do not, the world is likely to continue to degrade to a point where we truly cannot reverse

the trend or, worse, where we suffer catastrophic and traumatic events.[12]

Enter the book of Revelation. It comes to us from a different time and place. More important, it offers a radically different way of thinking and being in the world. It critiques unthinking patterns of cultural behavior and cherishes a different set of values. Ehrenfeld says that "we are stuck in a system that has created our dilemmas."[13] Revelation's bizarre visions and contemplation of an alternate future can help liberate us from our system and stimulate new thinking about ourselves and our world.

12. John R. Ehrenfeld, *Sustainability by Design: A Subversive Strategy for Transforming Our Consumer Culture* (New Haven, CT: Yale University Press, 2008), 20.
13. Ibid., 9.

Revelation's Personality

The Earth and the Future in an Apocalyptic Ecology

> "About this book of the Revelation of John, I leave everyone free to hold his own ideas . . . I say what I feel. I miss more than one thing in this book, and this makes me hold it to be neither apostolic or prophetic. . . . My spirit cannot fit itself into this book."[1]
> —Martin Luther

When we meet someone new, we size her or him up. What is the person like? What are her or his features, propensities, and habits? Does this person annoy us, entertain us? We ask: Is this someone we want to spend time with? In the quotation above, Martin Luther has found Revelation's personality unappealing. In this chapter we will acquaint ourselves with the book of Revelation by asking questions we might ask of a stranger: What is it like? What are its features? How does it present itself? Within the world of biblical scholarship, we call this type of investigation "exegesis." This is from a Greek word

---

1. Martin Luther, in the preface to his German Bible. As quoted in Judith Kovacs and Christopher Rowland, *Revelation*, Blackwell Bible Commentaries Series (Oxford: Blackwell, 2004), 44.

that literally means to "read out" the meaning of a text. Exegesis pays close attention to the details, forms, and features of a biblical text in order to come to an understanding of its author's aims and purposes. We will begin with broad contours, like observing someone's personality traits from across the room. We will then become increasingly focused—looking for the kind of depth that emerges from an engrossing dialogue—as we explore Revelation's personality in relation to ecological concerns.

First, we will summarize Revelation and its content. Then, we will ask six questions of Revelation, the answers to which will help us as we try to interpret the book. Finally, we will look at Revelation's view of the future, one in which God creates a new heaven and a new earth. Can such a vision of the future be helpful in caring for the environment? In the end, I hope to show that Revelation is interesting and worth reading, and that we can find a way, unlike Martin Luther, for it to fit with our spirits.

I. Introductions: A First Encounter with Revelation

When I was young my youth pastor told me that I shouldn't read Revelation until I had read and understood the rest of the Bible. If that were the point of entry, who could ever give it a try? Revelation is probably the most misunderstood book in the Bible. A quick YouTube search on "Revelation" spits back a ghastly array of doomsday predictions and opportunities to donate money. For most Christians, Revelation is probably the least read book in the New Testament. It is certainly intricate and unfamiliar, but once we acquaint ourselves with some of its features and convictions, its message is not that complicated.

Revelation will not hurt you. Ignore the advice of my youth pastor and read it. Forget that you are reading "THE BIBLE" and experience Revelation as a piece of literature. Know from the outset that its plot and message might be hard to follow. It is full of visions and symbolism that may be lost on our ears twenty centuries after it was written. Yet its seemingly illogical presentation is part of its power. The apocalypse is meant to resonate at an emotional, not an intellectual, level. Its personality is vivid and visionary; it's

The Hunger Games meets *Game of Thrones*. Let yourself enjoy it. I begin with a brief overview of its content so readers have some idea of what to expect.

Chapter 1 introduces the book as an "apocalypse." The author introduces himself in the first person (1:9) and says he was on the island of Patmos. John sees an opening vision and is directed to write down what he sees.

Chapters 2 and 3 contain letters that John writes to seven churches. These churches are clustered in the western parts of the Roman province of Asia (what we today might call Asia Minor), in modern-day Turkey. The letters show that these communities experienced a variety of religious and social struggles (for example, Rev 2:2, 9-10), and in many cases faced persecution or death (2:13-14).

Chapters 4 and 5 provide the first expansive vision of heaven and its throne. This vision contains elements that recur throughout Revelation. Twenty-four elders surround the throne, along with four living creatures. Note the detail with which these creatures are described (4:6-11); we will discuss the symbolism of such visions below. The elders and the creatures worship God constantly. In chapter 5 we meet the lamb, who has been slaughtered and whose blood has won victory and deserves praise.

Chapters 6 and 7 describe the seven seals. Revelation is fond of cycles of seven (there are seven seals, trumpets, and bowls of wrath). Each of the first four seals sets loose a horse and rider, each of which is given dominion to destroy the earth in various ways (such as with swords, famine, or wild animals). The remaining seals throw the entire cosmos into turmoil: the sun, moon, and stars are all darkened. People flee to the mountains from the greatness of God's fury and wrath (6:15-17).

Chapters 8 to 11 move to seven trumpets, each of which unleashes further devastation. One third of the earth is burned up (8:6-7); one third of the sea became like blood, killing its creatures (8:8-9); waters are polluted and made bitter by a falling star (8:10-11); and the sun, moon, and stars are dimmed. The fourth and fifth trumpets have more expansive consequences, with a smoky pit spewing frightening war-like locusts (9:1-12). The sixth trumpet releases four angels, along with two hundred million cavalry, whose job it is to kill one third of humanity. The blowing of the seventh trumpet brings this section to a close (11:5-19), after which loud voices in heaven declare God's sovereignty and proclaim that the time has come to destroy those who destroy the earth (11:18).

Chapters 12 to 14 interrupt the first two cycles of seven (seals and trumpets) to narrate war in heaven. A pregnant woman clothed with the sun appears to John. A dragon chases her, but she and her child escape. After this, war breaks out in heaven (12:7) between Michael and the angels and the dragon. This dragon is clearly identified with "the Devil and Satan" (12:9). When the dragon realizes he will not be able to destroy the woman and her son (protected by a personified earth that swallows up the dragon's water), he wages war on God's people on earth instead (12:17). Chapter 13 describes two beasts, the first on the seashore and a second that arises from the earth. They are given authority by the dragon and they control the earth. The second beast is particularly devious. He receives a mortal wound, yet survives. He controls all economic interactions, and without his mark no one can buy or sell anything. His number is 666.

Chapters 15 and 16 return to a cycle of seven, this time with bowls of wrath that are poured out on the earth. The impact of these bowls recalls earlier parts of Revelation, but they were also inspired by the plagues God sent on Egypt in the book of Exodus: for example, water turns to blood, darkness covers the earth. After the seventh bowl is poured out, a voice from the throne in the temple (implying it is the voice of God) says, "It is done!" (16:17). This proves to be true, as the rest of Revelation turns to the final destruction of evil and the creation of a new heaven and new earth.

Chapters 17 to 20 begin by describing a woman, drunk with the blood of the saints, riding on the beast. She is the great city that rules over all the kings, and she and the beast are destined for destruction. In chapter 18 a long poetic section revels in the destruction of Babylon, clearly meant to be understood as Rome. Part of the song rejoices over Rome's fall, but part of it gives voice to those segments of humanity—particularly the rich and powerful (18:11-19)—who lament over the city's destruction. In chapter 19 heaven rejoices and a white horse arrives with the power to win. An angel, along with an army of birds, destroys the beast and his army. The evil entities are thrown into the lake of fire and the birds gorge themselves on their flesh. After this the dead are judged. Anyone whose name is not written in the book will be doomed to the lake of fire (20:15).

Chapters 21 and 22 describe the new heaven and the new earth that God will create. The first heaven and earth "had passed away" (21:1). There is no more sea. A new Jerusalem descends from heaven to earth. God will dwell in this city with humanity. There will be no more death, tears will be wiped away, and mourning and pain will be no more (21:4). The new Jerusalem is described as having been built with a dizzying array of precious metals and stones. Through the city flows the river of life and on its banks grows a tree, the fruit of which will feed and heal all the nations. There will be no need for lamps or a sun, for God will provide light to all.

This has been only a very brief summary of some of the key episodes of Revelation. As this book progresses, we will engage many parts of John's writing in greater detail. We will not, however, be able to solve every problem or answer every question.

II. Small Talk: Six Questions for a Cocktail Party

It will help our investigation of Revelation to have some introduction to its key features and components. Here I present six questions we should ask about Revelation. Such information about date, time, place, and context are important components of exegesis. Knowing as much as we can about a book and its author will help us understand and interpret its personality.

1. WHO WROTE REVELATION
AND WHEN WAS IT WRITTEN?

Someone named "John" claims to have written the book of Revelation (1:4, 9). This is not the same John who wrote the gospel and three "letters" associated with that name in the New Testament. There are too many differences between the gospel and letters of John and Revelation to conclude that they stem from the same author. Who, then, was this John who wrote Revelation? We do not really know. Nevertheless, throughout this book, I will use "John" as a reference to the author of Revelation.

John says that he was an exile on the Island of Patmos (Rev 1:9). This island, today part of Greece, is close to the western coast of Asia Minor (modern-day Turkey), about fifty miles from ancient Ephesus. Was John really on Patmos? Maybe, maybe not. There is no convincing evidence that Patmos functioned as a regular place of exile or punishment in the ancient world, despite what some scholars have claimed.[2] John may have fled there on his own or been forced to live there for a while. It is also possible that John went there as part of his prophetic preaching.[3] On the other hand, John may never have been on Patmos at all. Other ancient apocalyptic literature is replete with mythological and symbolic geography.[4] Patmos could just be a literary feature of Revelation—an imagined rocky outpost in the sea where John received his wild visions.[5]

Most scholars would agree, however, that Revelation was written somewhere in the vicinity of Patmos. The churches addressed in the opening chapters are all located in Asia Minor, a region to which Patmos is adjacent. In addition, many of the ways in which Revelation addresses the Roman Empire would have found concrete expression in that part of the world (we will explore some of these

2. David E. Aune, *Revelation 1–5*, WBC 52A (Grand Rapids, MI: Zondervan, 1997), 75–81.

3. Ian Boxall, *Patmos in the Reception History of the Apocalypse* (Oxford: Oxford University Press, 2013), 19–22.

4. Ibid., 20.

5. Ibid., 15.

details in chapter three).[6] Beyond this broad geographical area, it is impossible to be more precise.

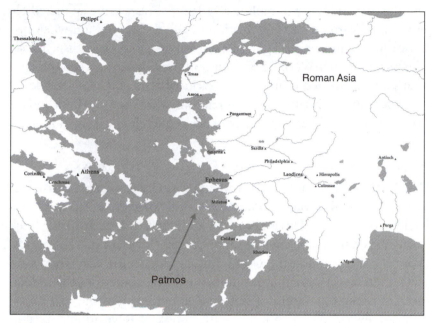

The Roman province of Asia at the time of the book of Revelation showing the location of the Island of Patmos. Map adapted from Accordance by Oak Tree Software. Used by permission.

When was this mostly anonymous, geographically ambiguous book written? The answer, if you have not picked up the theme yet, is: "We are not sure." John claims to have shared in persecution and to have had "patient endurance" (Rev 1:9). Because of this, Revelation has sometimes been coordinated with the reign of Emperor Nero (54–68 CE), whose torture of Christians was legendary. More recently, however, scholars have tended to place the book later in the first century, during the reign of Emperor Domitian (81–96 CE). We have evidence for sporadic persecution of Christians during this time

6. Steven J. Friesen, *Imperial Cults and the Apocalypse of John: Reading Revelation in the Ruins* (Oxford: Oxford University Press, 2001).

period as well.[7] The evidence needed to reach a specific conclusion on the date is, according to one scholar, "mixed" at best.[8]

Discussions about authorship, date, and place of composition bring out the best and worst in biblical scholars. Scholars bring an incredible amount of learning and information to the discussion, and when historical information sheds light on a biblical text, it can be indispensable. Whether written in 68 or 92, for our purposes we can proceed thinking that someone named John wrote a visionary work in the last decades of the first century. This work was written somewhere in Asia Minor and responds to the Christian experience of persecution in the Roman Empire.

2. WHAT DOES THE WORD "APOCALYPSE" MEAN?

The book of Revelation is also known by its Greek name, the "Apocalypse." In English today, we use the word "apocalypse" to mean the "end of the world." This is not really what the word means. The Greek word ἀποκάλυψις (*apokalypsis*) simply means "revelation." The apocalypse is not the end of the world, but a lifting of the veil, when God decides to reveal something to humanity. The content of this revelation, in ancient literature of this type, often includes the end times, but not always. As an apocalypse, the book of Revelation describes a scenario in which God reveals something to a human recipient (in our case, a man named John). An angel often mediates or interprets the revelation. When reading Revelation our question always must be "What is being revealed?" not "What is going to happen?"

Many people refer to John's Apocalypse as "Revelations." THIS IS WRONG. The word "apocalypse" is singular. When talking about this book, there should never be an "S" at the end. I often give my students this multiple-choice question on their final exam:

> The last book in the New Testament is:
>   a. Revelations
>   b. Mark
>   c. Irrelevant
>   d. Revelation

---

7. Aune, *Revelation 1–5*, lxvi–lxviii.

8. Ibid., lxix. Aune is also careful to document the ways in which the final form of Revelation that we read today may be a composite of originally independent sources that derive from various points of time in the first century.

The correct answer is "d." Getting the name wrong threatens our interpretation. Although this book has many visions, it has only one revelation: that Jesus is Lord and God is in control of the universe and its destiny. In its own words: "The kingdom of the world has become the kingdom of our Lord and of his Messiah, and he will reign forever and ever" (Rev 11:15). Jesus' lordship is the one revelation. Adding an "S" also does not heed the warning at the book's very end:

> I warn everyone who hears the words of the prophecy of this book: if anyone adds to them, God will add to that person the plagues described in this book. (Rev 22:18)

Just to be on the safe side, never put an "S" at the end.[9] Because "Apocalypse" means "Revelation," these two titles can be used interchangeably to refer to the book written by John.

3. IS REVELATION UNIQUE IN THE ANCIENT WORLD?

The book of Revelation is not unique. Many communities in ancient Judaism and Christianity produced apocalyptic literature. The Old Testament has one fully apocalyptic text, the book of Daniel. In the ancient world, communities of faith did not have rigid fences around what was "Scripture" and what was not. Texts that today we consider outside the Bible were important and many were apocalyptic. An anthology of apocalyptic literature, called *1 Enoch,* provides a wealth of background for the New Testament and Revelation in particular. The community that wrote the Dead Sea Scrolls was very apocalyptic and wrote many pieces of revelatory literature. Many of these earliest Jewish apocalyptic texts find their origins in the Hellenistic period (approximately 300–50 BCE) and the experience of Greek culture, antagonistic kings, and oppression and violence.

The years 66–70 in the first century CE saw a war between the Jews and the Romans. At the end of the war, the Romans destroyed the temple in Jerusalem, which many Jews interpreted as a cataclysmic event. The cognitive dissonance and struggle that resulted from

---

9. I borrow this "joke" from Brian Blount, with his permission.

this war and destruction led to more Jewish apocalyptic writing. Two texts in particular, *2 Baruch* and *4 Ezra*, are apocalypses that share many features with the book of Revelation. They struggle with the problem of evil, expressed through visions, angelic interpretations, and revelations about God and the future.

A famous biblical scholar, Rudolf Bultmann, once asked: Is Apocalypticism the mother of Christian theology?[10] The answer is "yes." Jesus himself seems to have viewed the world as having run its course. His first public statement in the Gospel of Mark suggests as much: "The time is fulfilled, and the kingdom of God has come near" (Mark 1:15). The earliest writer in the New Testament, the apostle Paul, held an apocalyptic worldview (see Gal 1:4, 11-12; Rom 8:1-30). 2 Peter envisions a future destruction of the world (3:11-13). Revelation, within the ancient world broadly and the New Testament specifically, is not alone in its apocalyptic view of history.

We cannot read apocalyptic literature in a vacuum, ignorant of the times in which it was produced, the style employed, and the themes it espouses. Imagine watching an episode of "Survivor" if you had no concept of reality television. Imagine our confusion if we were to read a Harry Potter book and had never read a novel. The more we know about what we read the better situated we will be to understand what we read. Knowing something about apocalyptic literature written before and during Revelation's own time period proves indispensable in understanding that book's features and emphases.

4. DOES REVELATION PREDICT THE FUTURE?

I suspect that a majority of people in the United States, if asked, would agree vaguely that the book of Revelation intends to predict the future. A recent Public Religion Research Institute poll found that 15 percent of Americans think the events in the book of Reve-

---

10. Rudolf Bultmann, "Ist die Apokalyptik die Mutter der christlichen Theologie?" in *Apophoreta: Festschrift für Ernst Haenchen*, ed. Walter Eltester and Franz H. Kettler (Berlin: Töpelmann, 1964), 64–69.

lation will come true *in their lifetime*.[11] A different poll found that, when asked if we are living in the end times "as described by the prophecies in the Bible," 41 percent of people said "yes."[12] Having such a worldview could drastically impact your view of history. There is significant evidence, for example, that a literal understanding of biblical prophecies shaped George W. Bush's foreign policy.[13] At a facile level, such readings of Revelation make sense. The book certainly presents many scenarios of what will happen in the future. Such predictions, however, were not John's true intention. This literature emerges in a specific time and place, written to grapple with and interpret a present moment. Understanding how and why Revelation does not predict the future is the biggest hurdle facing its modern interpreters. I offer here two brief examples that will demonstrate this point.

Revelation begins (chaps. 2–3) with letters that John sends to seven churches. These letters hint at specific sociological circumstances that prompt their writing. They refer to opponents and groups of false prophets (2:2-6). They struggle with the problem of eating food sacrificed to idols (2:15), a question of social and religious identity for early Christian monotheism. In the letter to Pergamum, it says: "You are holding fast to my name, and you did not deny your faith in me even in the days of Antipas my witness, my faithful one, who was killed among you, where Satan lives" (Rev 2:13). These words refer obliquely to a real circumstance: someone named Antipas was killed. As we will continue to explore in later chapters, the community to which Revelation was written was likely experiencing severe challenges related to their vulnerable position in the Roman Empire. In certain situations, local populations could be asked to participate in public sacrifices that were part of

11. Public Religion Research Institute Online: http://publicreligion.org /research/2012/12/prri-rns-december-2012-survey.

12. Religion Press Release Services Online: http://pressreleases.religion news.com/2013/09/11/shock-poll-startling-numbers-of-americans-believe -world-now-in-the-end-times.

13. Michael Orlov Grossman and Ronald Eric Matthews Jr., *Perspectives on the Legacy of George W. Bush* (Newcastle upon Tyne: Cambridge Scholars Publishing, 2008), 124–26.

the polytheistic religions of the day. Some Christians refused to participate and it cost them their lives. Revelation reveals that God has not abandoned these people. It copes with the present and does not predict the future.

Revelation is perhaps most famous for the number 666. Chapter 13 discusses the second of two beasts:

> Then I saw another beast that rose out of the earth; it had two horns like a lamb and it spoke like a dragon . . . This calls for wisdom: let anyone with understanding calculate the number of the beast, for it is the number of a person. Its number is six hundred sixty-six. (Rev 13:11, 18)

In my own anecdotal experience, the mark of the beast (666) has been distributed to Mikhail Gorbachev, George W. Bush, Barack Obama, and Pope Francis. Any such attempt to identify the beast is ignorant of John's true intention. John used an ancient form of numerology called "Gamatria," which assigns numerical value to letters and words. If the Greek form of Nero Caesar is transliterated into Hebrew as קסר נרון, then the numerical value becomes 666.[14] The number represents Nero, a figure to whom John alludes in 13:14, where the beast is said to have survived a mortal wound. (There were ancient traditions about Nero just like this—that he had died and come back to life.[15]) Nero was notorious among Christians because he blamed them for causing the fire that destroyed Rome in 64 CE. He lit them on fire and threw them to wild animals. For the original reader of Revelation the identity of the beast, marked by the number 666, was not in doubt: it was Nero. Any attempt to coordinate the number 666 and the beast with a later figure, be it political leader or Roman Catholic pontiff, completely misses the point.

The book of Revelation was written in the specific context of the Roman Empire. This context posed serious challenges to the Chris-

14. See David E. Aune, *Revelation 6–16*, WBC 52B (Grand Rapids, MI: Zondervan, 1998), 770.

15. See ibid., 737–40. See also Hans-Josef Klauck, "Do They Never Come Back? Nero Redivivus and the Apocalypse of John," *Catholic Biblical Quarterly* 63, no. 4 (2001): 683–98.

tian community, challenges that were social, theological, political, and economic. Any attempt to make Revelation relevant to today must first understand its rootedness in its original time and place. We will look at some details of this Roman context in depth in chapter three, understanding it as John's "upbringing" in a specific context.

5. HOW DOES REVELATION COMMUNICATE ITS MESSAGE?

I wrote earlier that Revelation is not that hard to understand. That may not be entirely true. I went to school for nine years of my life in order to be able to help explain it to people. But there is hope. If we want to have some insight into its personality, it may be helpful to explore some of its methods in order to comprehend it.

a. Symbolism

Revelation communicates frequently through symbolism. When my students encounter the dragon in Revelation 12, they immediately ask: "What does it symbolize?" They know (at least I think they do) that dragons are not real, and so the author must intend some significance behind the dragon that is separate from literal history. Very little of John's Apocalypse is meant to be taken literally. Dragons, trumpets, bowls of wrath, earthquakes, and mail-clad locusts are part of John's symbolic universe. Because of our chronological distance from John, his symbolism might confuse us. Some of it comes from the Old Testament, some of it from his context of the Roman Empire. Some of it comes from the traditions and liturgical celebrations already in place within early Christianity.

For example, in Revelation 7:14 John refers to those who have "washed their robes and made them white in the blood of the Lamb." This image makes no logical sense. Putting blood on a robe will not make it white. What is important here is the symbolism: the image of Jesus's blood as that which makes things new. The symbol of Jesus as a slaughtered lamb stands at the heart of John's apocalypse. John offers an image of defeat and weakness as that which ultimately will conquer.

Much of the symbolism in Revelation relates to its Roman context. John puts symbols of Rome's economic and military power into the hands of the four horsemen (Rev 6:1-8). The involvement of the sun, moon, and stars in Revelation makes sense in a context where the Roman emperors coordinated their reigns with celestial bodies. The symbolism in chapter 17 makes clear that the woman riding on the beast should be understood as Rome: the woman is "the great city that rules over the kings of the earth" (Rev 17:18).

John also uses symbolic numbers. He repeatedly employs the number 12 or multiples of it (24, 144,000). This number has a connection to the Old Testament in the twelve tribes of the Israelites, a link that John makes explicit in Revelation 21:12. The number 12 also evokes the twelve apostles (see Rev 21:14). The number 7 is prominent. John presents seven lamp stands (1:12); seven letters to seven churches (2:1–3:22); and seven seals, trumpets, and bowls of wrath. We have already coordinated the number 666 with Nero, but thinking about that number's symbolism could highlight additional meaning. Brian Blount points out that John's obsession with the number 7 ought to tell us something also about his use of the number 6. The number 7 was known in the ancient world to represent wholeness or completeness, which could explain John's emphasis of it. The number 666 is the beast's flailing attempts to reach the completeness of God and the lamb, but never quite able to make it. To quote Blount:

> It is as though [the beast] is struggling to become something it never can be. In that regard, its own name betrays its limitation. Even as it flaunts its strength, it wallows in weakness. It is always a six, never a seven; 666 on into eternity. It will never have complete power because, like the number that symbolizes it, it will never itself be completely whole.[16]

John's symbolism is frequently problematic for a modern audience. For instance, John's use of feminine imagery perpetuates misogyny.[17] Women in the book are either harlots and whores or pure

---

16. Brian K. Blount, *Revelation: A Commentary* (Louisville, KY: Westminster John Knox, 2009), 262.

17. Tina Pippin, *Death and Desire: The Rhetoric of Gender in the Apocalypse of John* (Louisville, KY: Westminster John Knox Press, 1992). See also the critiques in Catherine Keller, *Apocalypse Now and Then: A Feminist Guide to the End of the World* (Boston: Beacon Press, 1996).

brides.[18] The Apocalypse is also very violent, relying upon images of armies, weapons, disease, and death.[19] Finally, for our present concerns, the treatment of the earth and sea in Revelation also conjures its own type of symbolism. What does it do to an environmental ethic when chapter upon chapter portrays an environment engulfed by cataclysm?

These brief observations scratch only the surface of John's symbolism. In order to interpret the Apocalypse properly, we must understand how its author builds meaning. For John, one of his primary methods is to use symbols and metaphors to communicate his point. John never intended that there, literally, will be a dragon, a whore, or blood as deep as a horse's bridle. Exegesis seeks to understand, with as much precision as possible, what the symbol meant in John's context before applying it to our world today.

b. The Jewish Scriptures

John's Apocalypse could not exist without the Jewish Scriptures. One scholar has summarized the whole of the Apocalypse by saying that it is a "reconstruction of the Exodus at the heart of the Roman empire."[20] John knew these sacred texts in Greek translation and interacts with and emulates them in nearly every episode of Revelation. In 1:3 John calls his work a "prophecy." He indeed is conversant with prophetic traditions of Israel. His repeated visions of the heavenly throne draw from many parts of Isaiah and Ezekiel. Beasts rising from the sea and language about the Son of Man disclose influence from the book of Daniel. In several visions, particularly those that envisage destruction and punishment on the earth, the story of the Exodus provides precedent, an event Israel flexibly applied to a variety of historical events in its history (for example, return from exile seen in Isaiah 51:9-11). The vision of a new Jerusalem built

18. See Barbara R. Rossing, *The Choice Between Two Cities: Whore, Bride, and Empire in the Apocalypse* (Harrisburg, PA: Trinity Press International, 1999).

19. The violence of Revelation has long been seen as a problem for the book's interpretation. See Blount, *Revelation*, 1–5; René Girard, *Battling to the End: Conversations with Benoit Chantre* (East Lansing: Michigan State University Press, 2009).

20. Pablo Richard, *Apocalypse: A People's Commentary on the Book of Revelation* (Maryknoll, NY: Orbis Books, 1995), 4–5.

with precious stones finds analogs in a variety of biblical texts, such as Isaiah 54, Ezekiel 28, and Tobit 13. The Psalms offer examples of the types of hymns of praise that punctuate John's text.

John's influences are not limited only to those things that we think of as being in the "Old Testament." In John's day, such an authoritative boundary around sacred texts did not exist. Other texts, such as *1 Enoch, Jubilees,* and parts of the Dead Sea Scrolls, while they may or may not have influenced John directly, give us an understanding of the literature and its thought patterns in the ancient world, and will often prove illuminating in understanding John's intentions.

One of the challenges for modern readers of Revelation is that we often find ourselves much less familiar with Israel's Scriptures than John or his readers would have been. Allusions fall on deaf ears. Motifs and visions lose their depth if their intended intertextual resonance gets missed. These intertextual links will prove indispensable as we explore John's ecological personality.

6. HOW ARE WE SUPPOSED TO READ
THE BOOK OF REVELATION?

Imagine you pick up a book with no cover and start reading it. Within a few minutes you encounter a dragon, darkened stars, and blood covering the earth. Such unrealistic images might allow you to guess what kind of literature you were reading: fantasy or some type of fiction. Making such a judgment will produce a series of assumptions about what to expect in this type of literature and how to interpret it. One of the interesting things about the book of Revelation is that it forces the reader to be conscious of how she or he will interpret. Reading Revelation is not like reading a seemingly transparent narrative about Jesus in one of the gospels. Revelation's bizarre imagery and eschatological message force the reader to think about *how* to it ought to be interpreted. We call this a "hermeneutic," from the Greek word *hermeneia* meaning "interpretation." Revelation requires a hermeneutical posture, a strategy for interpretation.

The field of biblical studies has long been dominated by a reading strategy called the "historical-critical method." This approach prioritized history and sought the mind of the author. According to this approach, the more we can learn about the historical world in which the author lived, the better we can pin down what the author originally intended to convey. In the last thirty years or so, the assumptions of the historical-critical method have come under scrutiny. It was primarily a white-European-male reading strategy. Scholars increasingly have become more upfront about their hermeneutic; they approach biblical texts from consciously feminist, postcolonial, or womanist perspectives.

The last twenty years have seen great interest in another hermeneutical approach. "Ecological hermeneutics" intentionally reads the Bible in light of our modern ecological situation. For example, a series of books called "The Earth Bible Project" attempts to read the Bible from the perspective of the earth.[21] These authors start with a set of six "ecojustice" principles on which their reading of the Bible will be based. Some scholars prefer not to start with ecojustice principles, but nevertheless attempt to read biblical texts for their environmental import.[22]

My own approach has been informed by, and will utilize, many different methodologies. At times, the historical-critical method will prove essential in determining the literature John inherited and the political and environmental situation in which he lived. I will also draw from various authors who consciously practice ecological hermeneutics. I also find help from the field of ecocriticism. Ecocriticism derives from literary criticism, defined as "reading with attention to treatments of nature, land, and place, informed by a desire to understand past and present connections between literature and human attitudes regarding the earth."[23] Adopting such an approach, scholars investigate literature such as Chaucer, medieval Spanish hagiography, and early German poetry, in order to understand the ecological consciousness of people in various times and places.[24] This

21. Norman C. Habel, ed., *Readings from the Perspective of Earth* (Sheffield: Sheffield Academic Press, 2000).

22. David Horrell, *Bible and the Environment: Towards a Critical Ecological Biblical Theology* (London: Equinox Publishing, 2010).

23. From Rebecca Douglass, as quoted in Connie Scarborough, ed., *Inscribing the Environment: Ecocritical Approaches to Medieval Spanish Literature* (Berlin: Walter de Gruyter, 2013), 2.

24. See the following: Sarah Stanbury, "Ecochaucer: Green Ethics and Medieval Nature," *The Chaucer Review* 39, no. 1 (2004): 1–16; Scarborough,

definition summarizes effectively my goal for reading Revelation. I seek how Revelation was shaped by its own experience of the land, both physically and through art, literature, and propaganda of the ancient world. At the same time, we will explore how Revelation has itself shaped the ecological imaginations of communities across the centuries. Such an eclectic approach will allow us to evaluate Revelation's role in shaping our modern situation, and also to craft an argument about its potential contribution in the future.

III. Engrossing Dialogue: Probing John's Ecological Personality

Now that we are acquainted with Revelation, we turn to one specific aspect of its personality: the problems and prospects it presents to those who read the Bible in the context of our modern environmental situation.

As we will see in subsequent chapters, humans created and noticed environmental problems in antiquity. Yet, our modern scientific age helps us understand them in a new way. Because of this, only in the last twenty or thirty years have scholars begun asking critical questions of biblical texts in light of what ecology tells us about our world. Even a quick perusal of Revelation suggests that it has a fascinating environmental personality. The entire cosmos is its stage, involving the earth, sun, moon, and stars. John's focus is very terrestrial, using the Greek word for "earth" (γῆ) eighty-two times, twice as many as the next closest book in the New Testament. Revelation also includes nonhuman life: birds, fish, horses, dogs, and locusts. Other animals (or parts of them) play roles in hybrid creatures with features similar to oxen, lions, scorpions, eagles, leopards, and many others. Specific plants also receive treatment, with references to grass, trees, barley, olives, grapes, and cinnamon.

Inscribing the Environment, and Christopher Clason, " 'Gebrochen bluomen unde gras': Medieval Ecological Consciousness in Selected Poems by Walther von der Vogelweide," in *Rural Space in the Middle Ages and Early Modern Age: The Spatial Turn in Premodern Studies*, ed. Albrecht Classen (Berlin: Walter de Gruyter, 2012), 227–50.

To be clear, John's myriad references to the cosmos, earth, sea, animals, and plants do not cohere into a beautiful pastoral montage. Quite the contrary. The earth and its inhabitants in Revelation experience the death throes of the end of an age. The earth convulses with God's wrath. Hail, earthquakes, and lightning punctuate the narrative, commonplace tropes of upheaval at the end of time (see, for example, Mark 13). God turns water, sun, and moon to blood, scorches the earth, and kills millions of humans and animals. It is not a pretty picture.

These features of Revelation's personality, along with their many details we have not yet discussed, might lead to skepticism about Revelation's potential contribution to an environmental ethic.[25] How could a book that so vividly describes the earth's destruction help its preservation? This question is not easy to answer. Some despair of ever trying. A colleague of mine who writes and teaches about environmental ethics recently said at a department meeting: "I don't give a damn about the Bible." He was joking, of course. But the comment is indicative of the perspective of many in his field. It is not uncommon for environmentalists to have little time for the Bible (and Revelation in particular) because its personality is so overtly negative. Does John depict destruction of the earth so negatively that we should avoid him, like an estranged friend whom we do not want to see anymore?

My aim in this book is twofold. First, I hope to show that there are contextual reasons that help explain why John's Apocalypse depicts destruction of the entire cosmos. There are reasons for his negativity. He is influenced by and emulating other apocalyptic literature, which often contains destruction aplenty (we will see an example of this in chapter 2). John's convulsing, smoking earth may be more *de*scriptive than it is *pre*scriptive. Second, I hope to show that John's environmental personality provides a positive contribution to environmental concerns. Thus, we want to understand John's ecological personality in two ways—both to understand why it looks

25. See, for instance, Michael Northcott, "Girard, Climate Change, and Apocalypse," in *Can We Survive Our Origins? Readings in René Girard's Theory of Violence and the Sacred*, ed. Pierpaolo Antonello and Paul Gifford, 287–309 (East Lansing: Michigan State University Press, 2015).

the way it does, but also to understand what it could be, to unlock its potential contributions.

Having given this broad introduction to John's ecological personality, we will look closely at one specific aspect of that personality: his view of the future and the pitfalls and prospects it provides for an apocalyptic ecology.

We begin our deep exploration of John's ecological personality at the end. In chapter 21, John sees a new heaven and a new earth. God will dwell among humans and there will be an end to death, mourning, crying, and pain because the "first things have passed away" (21:4). Jerusalem descends, made of precious stones and exceedingly immense. The sun, moon, and stars are no longer necessary because God will provide light directly (21:22-25). Things are so new there will be neither mourning nor morning. The details corroborate nicely the voice from the throne: "see, I am making all things new" (21:5).

From an environmental point of view, John's visions present a problem. If there is no continuity between our world and the future world that descends, then there is little reason to care for the world today. Many Christians today read the end of Revelation in a way that is escapist, that God is coming to rescue us from this present world.[26] Our destiny lies with God and God's new creation, so why should we bother with the fate of the original?

1. RENEWAL AND CONTINUITY

One way to solve the problem of Revelation's eschatology is to try to find in the text hints of continuity between the present and future. In the view of many scholars, John intends just this. John, in their view, does not envision complete destruction; his eschatology should be understood as "renewal" or "transformation" rather than complete re-creation. From an environmental point of view, this makes sense. If John intends continuity between old and new, then our actions

26. See some of the perspectives outlined in Barbara R. Rossing, "For the Healing of the World: Reading Revelation Ecologically," in *From Every People and Nation: The Book of Revelation in Intercultural Perspective*, ed. David Rhoads, 165–82 (Minneapolis: Fortress Press, 2005).

in the present age will have consequences carried over into the new. Such a view prevents us from disengaging from care for the earth by claiming that it's all going to get blown up anyway. This view emphasizes that God makes "all things new" not "all new things."[27]

There are good exegetical arguments in favor of a reading that emphasizes renewal. Barbara Rossing finds a similar view in Paul's letter to the Romans (8:18-25), in which all of creation is longing for redemption. She says: "the earth will become 'new' in the sense of resurrection or renewal, just as our bodies will be resurrected, brought to new life—and yet they are still our bodies."[28] She claims that John's use of the word "new" can mean "renewed" but "certainly does not mean a 'different' earth."[29] In Rossing's view, God intends to rescue the earth, not destroy it. Douglas Moo agrees with this assessment, calling the new creation in Revelation a "radical transformation" not annihilation.[30]

Mark Stephens buttresses the "renewal" reading by pointing out that John does not specify the mechanism of the first world's passing away; it is not thrown into the lake of fire like the beast, the prophet, and the devil (Rev 20:10). Stephens draws a parallel with Revelation 4:11, where the elders and creatures around the throne praise God for creating "all things" (Greek τὰ πάντα). Because all things are participants in God's creation and redemption, it "cannot be that the present creation is completely abolished or annihilated."[31]

The ecological payoff from such a reading of John's language is obvious. God desires to heal the world, not destroy it. Revelation then calls its readers to leave behind the present world right now and "live already in terms of God's vision for our new world."[32] In

---

27. Mark B. Stephens, *Annihilation or Renewal? The Meaning and Function of New Creation in the Book of Revelation* (Tübingen: Mohr Siebeck, 2011), 239, esp. n. 322. See also Douglas J. Moo, "Nature in the New Creation: New Testament Eschatology and the Environment," *Journal of the Evangelical Theological Society* 49, no. 3 (2006): 466, who makes a similar distinction.

28. Rossing, "For the Healing of the World," 170.

29. Ibid.

30. Moo, "Nature in the New Creation," 465.

31. Stephens, *Annihilation or Renewal*, 241. He coordinates John's perspective with several parts of the Old Testament in his argument as well.

32. Rossing, "For the Healing of the World," 172.

other words, continuity between present and future makes possible the ethical work of creating the new world in the present. Ethical behavior in the ecological realm will align oneself with God's aims. Revelation points out the exploitation of the earth and its people, and we must begin the work of ending that right away, rather than sitting around and waiting for God to do it in the future.

2. REVISITING ANNIHILATION

There is much to recommend the "renewal" proposal, but I do not find it totally convincing. Scholars who advocate for this position do so at the expense of details in Revelation that suggest complete annihilation of the cosmos. I want to consider a different point of view, one that suggests that John intends a complete break between the old and the new, and then see if we can find a way for this view also to be ecologically helpful.

a. Discontinuity between old and new

The language in Revelation emphasizes discontinuity more than continuity. Revelation 21:1 describes a "new heaven and a new earth" because the old earth had "passed away." The opening vision concludes with a summary: "the first things have passed away" (21:4). The order of the Greek words in 21:5 emphasizes newness. If we were to translate them very literally, it would read: "New I am making all things." The plain sense of these words suggests that God creates something radically new. John prepares his reader for such an idea in the previous chapter. In his scene of the last judgment, God sits on the white throne and "the earth and the heaven fled from his presence, and no place was found for them" (20:11).

In addition, the new world that John goes on to describe shows little continuity with the old. The new Jerusalem's scale is not imaginable (144,000 square stadia) and made with such a variety of stones and precious metals as to be completely unrealistic. Moreover, the new creation has no basis in physical or biological reality. There is no sun, moon, or stars. God will light the world directly (21:23). Night will never come. One river and one tree will feed and nourish everyone. The future is urban, with no animals, wild places, wilderness, or countryside. In short, the new earth seems decisively new; the details show scant continuity with the old.[33] I find little evidence in chapters 21 and 22 for the former earth's persistence in the new creation.

b. God as Pantokrator

As we discussed above, Mark Stephens turns to Revelation 4:11 and the praise of God for having "created all things" as justification for persistence of the old in the new creation. It suggests "renovation and renewal" and not a complete discarding of the old.[34] This evidence could be read differently. Revelation certainly praises God for creation. In 5:13 all of creation raises its voice in praise. In 15:3 God's mighty deeds are praised. One of the common epithets used for God throughout Revelation is the Greek word *pantokrator* (παντοκράτωρ)—God all-powerful or omnipotent. John demonstrates the appropriateness of this word through God's control of the universe, especially the elements of creation—hail, wind, fire, beasts, and birds. A completely new creation reinforces the idea of God as *pantokrator* (omnipotent) better than a God who only renews. It is God's role as all-powerful creator that is praised consistently throughout Revelation; one would expect the creation at the end to be commensurate with that theme. If so, we might expect a totally new creation, one where God has made all new things.

c. Complete annihilation of Rome

If God only renews the earth and does not completely destroy it, it would diminish John's critique of the Roman Empire. We will deal more fully with John's Roman context in chapter three, but John's primary impetus for writing was to critique the dominance of Rome. John intends to show that God truly is in control and that Rome will

---

33. The things used to build the new Jerusalem are made from known materials. The statement in Revelation 21:26 about people bringing into the city the "glory and honor of the nations" could also hint at continuity, although the idea of the nations gathered in the new city is common in some prophetic literature. I think, however, that Moo overstates the case when saying that Revelation 21–22 is "full" of references to the original creation ("Nature in the New Creation," 466). The fact that the new creation contains recognizable elements does not necessarily indicate continuity with the old.

34. Stephens, *Annihilation or Renewal*, 239.

come to an end. The earth—actually, the entire cosmos—has become Rome's domain, which is why it unfortunately bears the brunt of so much of God's punishment. Revelation doesn't seek to destroy the earth, but because the earth has become Rome's, it becomes a casualty in the apocalyptic war. Anything less than total destruction would not meet the challenge of the extent to which Rome has infected the earth. Like treatment of a foot with gangrene, John does not apply a poultice that might heal the infection. He amputates.

d. Precedent in Israel's Scriptures

Finally, there is precedent in Jewish literature and traditions that envisioned a destruction of the universe.[35] The beginning verses of Revelation 21 are patterned on several texts from the book of Isaiah. Isaiah 65:17 offers a similar distinction between the first heaven and the first earth that could have influenced John. In addition, the phrase "I am making all things new" in 21:5 is likely influenced by Isaiah 43:19, where it says, "behold, I am doing a new thing" (author's translation). According to Edward Adams, such language "implies that God's eschatological creative activity corresponds to his original creative act."[36] It is clear from the context that the new creation in Revelation is not creation *ex nihilo* (from nothing), which was probably not even available in the thought world of the day.[37] Given what we know from John's influences, the language indicates a "cosmic dissolution" that precedes a "new creative act."[38] John envisions the end of the world in a "fully cosmic and destructionist sense."[39]

Barbara Rossing, in arguing for continuity and renewal, says: "the God of Revelation does not seek to destroy the earth. Rather, God seeks to rescue the earth from the empire that is devastating

---

35. To be clear, finding precedent in previous Jewish literature cannot settle the question. The evidence presents examples of both annihilation and renewal. See Moo, "Nature in the New Creation," 465n60. See also the exhaustive study in Edward Adams, *The Stars Will Fall from Heaven: Cosmic Catastrophe in the New Testament and Its World*, LNTS 347 (London: T&T Clark, 2007), 25–129.

36. Adams, *The Stars will Fall from Heaven*, 237.

37. Ibid., 238.

38. Ibid., 238.

39. Ibid., 239.

it—the land, the seas, and the creatures who inhabit them—so that creation can be brought to fulfillment."[40] I agree that the God of Revelation does not want to destroy the earth. But that fact alone does not mean that God will not do it. The sea and the creatures to which she refers have no place in the new creation; even the sea was no more (21:1). It seems quite possible that God's creative power and thorough critique of Rome manifest themselves in Revelation as destruction of the old and a completely new creation.

3. BOTH "ANNIHILATION" AND "RENEWAL"

In the end, I am wary of either/or dichotomies when reading biblical texts. Sometimes there is a right and a wrong answer. In this case, a binary approach to the annihilation or renewal debate is not warranted. I am concerned that those who read Revelation ecologically turn too quickly to "renewal," at the expense of taking seriously the details that support "annihilation." It seems clear that we should read John's future as having elements of both annihilation and renewal; either of these categories in isolation would be "inadequate."[41] John's text is symbolic, apocalyptic, often poetic, and rarely straightforward. It is never meant to be literal, which means we are not forced to choose one of these two options. John seems to want to have it both ways: the earth will be annihilated, but some parts of it will be renewed.

A both/and approach will prove extremely helpful in finding an apocalyptic ecology in the end of Revelation. The continuity that John envisions empowers the inhabitants of the earth. Those who endure to the end, whose names are written in the book, will be spared destruction and will find life in the new creation. Such continuity is essential for any ethics to be wrung from the Apocalypse. If there is *nothing* we can do now to change our fate in the future, then there is no impetus for right moral action. John's profile of Rome's greed and its ecological destruction suggests that avoiding Rome's sins (18:4) would have a significant ecological component.

---

40. Rossing, "For the Healing of the World," 175.

41. Craig R. Koester, *Revelation: A New Translation with Introduction and Commentary*, AB 38A (New Haven, CT: Yale University Press, 2014), 803.

The actions of humanity will, to some extent, determine their fate in the future creation, placing an environmental mandate on humanity.

On the other hand, we must notice how extremely new the new creation is. The end of the sea and an entirely new earth put a poignant end to Rome's dominion. The new world is so new that it does not run according to known natural laws. The new also eschews the laws of economics. At the center of the future city one finds a river and a tree, which are available freely to everyone. God provides for all with no need for old economic structures. As Rossing says, the details of the new creation, with its open gates, free food and water, and its healing tree of life, invite "us to imagine our world differently."[42] I agree, except that this is not an image of "our" world. It is a vision of a future world that bears little resemblance to our own. Emphasizing the annihilation of the old will help us to see how radically new this vision is. The edifice of human civilization and its destruction of the earth impede this new world. This new world cannot come into existence without the dismantling of the old one. To speak of John's future world only in terms of renewal and continuity makes it too easy to dismiss how radically new it really is. The new earth created by God is ecologically unrecognizable to us.

The new heaven and new earth in Revelation are both continuous with, but also a break from, our world today. If this is true, some helpful environmental components emerge because it creates a role for both God and humanity. If there is no continuity, then humans just sit back, watch, and wait. Continuity necessitates an active human role in rejecting the greed and dominance of the world's order and its ecological impact and requires living in a different way. On the other hand, the annihilation and completely new creation retain an important theological element of John's vision of the future. A Christian environmentalism will be in trouble if it becomes nothing more than a human endeavor. It must always begin with recognition and praise of God as creator. God's creative prowess is not only retrospective; God is not limited by what God has done in the past. We should not think that God is going to create the literal world as described in Revelation. However, recognizing the clean break between the present and the future world keeps God free and unfet-

42. Rossing, "For the Healing of the World," 173.

tered for new creation. God can do what God wants in the future. The broad contours of the new world in Revelation could be environmentally positive. A future where resources are freely available (and not exploited for economic gain) and provide healing rather than division would indeed be a new world.

When discussing the drastic change necessary to create a truly sustainable world, John Ehrenfeld uses the term "transformation." This word helpfully encapsulates the vision of the future in Revelation. Something new is created, but it is built upon what already existed. He is careful to point out that we cannot achieve a sustainable ecological world if we view it as built on a sense of progress. The worldview that lingers from the enlightenment lies when it tells us we can build a better and better world. Progress and transformation are not the same things: "transformation implies an abrupt, discontinuous change."[43] Although John of Patmos does not dream about such transformation for ecological reasons, he does conjure the same need for transformation as leading thinkers on sustainability, like Ehrenfeld.

When read with elements of both annihilation and renewal, Revelation's eschatology offers something that scientific ecologists are increasingly short on: hope. God will not abandon the earth and its inhabitants. Such hope makes no sense in the context of a western scientific mentality. It is not a hope that my colleagues in the biology department can talk about. John's hope claims that the work of empire that destroys our world will not have the last word. God's creative power is not limited to setting the universe in motion and then walking away. God is the beginning and the end (Rev 1:8), is and always will be the creator. At the same time, this hope should not make us passive. As Walter Brueggemann says, "hope is a concrete summons to act in venturesome ways."[44] An apocalyptic ecology will claim God's role in the future and call believers to be the pioneers in that new world.

43. John R. Ehrenfeld, *Sustainability by Design* (New Haven, CT: Yale University Press, 2008), 66.

44. Walter Brueggemann, "Faith at the *Nullpunkt*," in *The End of the World and the Ends of God*, ed. John Polkinghorne and Michael Welker, 143–54 (Harrisburg, PA: Trinity Press International, 2000).

CHAPTER TWO

Revelation's Ancestors

An Ecological Alternative in the Context of Hellenistic War

> "We abuse land because we see it as a commodity belonging to us. When we see land as a community to which we belong, we may begin to use it with love and respect."
>
> —Aldo Leopold

In the year 332 BCE Alexander the Great swept through Jerusalem and its surrounding territory: a lightning war with a glacial impact. Although Jews had encountered the Greeks and their culture long before, the post-Alexander or Hellenistic age imposed Greek culture throughout the territories he conquered. The Hellenistic age presented a series of new challenges to the Jewish people: kings who made themselves divine; a Greek cultural and religious elitism that diminished ancient Jewish traditions; and constant war and violence. The Jews responded to these challenges in a variety of ways. Some found avenues to economic success while striving to remain culturally distinct. Some assimilated completely into the language and norms of Greek culture. But some resisted. In this chapter, we will examine this third group—a community of Jewish people who combined their past traditions and lived experience in order to concoct a type of resistance literature called "apocalyptic." These are among the "ancestors" of Revelation.

Meeting Revelation's ancestors will allow us to understand those things that the book inherited. In the context of seeking Revelation's environmental point of view, this will prove indispensable. Jewish apocalyptic literature is infused with creation and often its destruction. It also often envisions a cataclysmic end to the world in a way similar to Revelation. In this chapter, we will see a Jewish apocalyptic text that struggles with the destruction of creation. This literature responds by offering a different vision for what the natural world should be like, one featuring uncultivated wilderness. This "environmental alternative" is a critique of the way human institutions have destroyed God's creation. Understanding this precedent will help us contextualize and understand the details of how the book of Revelation depicts the natural environment and its theological interpretation of how history unfolds.

I. "What the . . . ?": Introducing *1 Enoch*

An obscure verse from the book of Genesis says: "Enoch walked with God; then he was no more, because God took him" (5:24). This image of Enoch snatched up to heaven fuels much speculation about him in later centuries. During the Hellenistic period an anthology of apocalyptic texts (called *1 Enoch*) focuses on Enoch and the things God revealed to him. This is crazy literature if you are not familiar with it. For example, it starts with a story about rebellious angels in heaven, also called "watchers," who conspire to leave heaven and impregnate the earth's women. The women then give birth to giants who destroy the earth—its plants and animals—and devour flesh and drink blood. Good angels become aware of this scenario and present the case before God. God dispatches these good angels to defeat the evil watchers, reserving terrible places of punishment for them.

When I teach this literature to my students I often get blank stares, or maybe an informal email that goes something like: "Why are we reading nonbiblical texts about giants and angels and stuff?" Although not biblical, literature like *1 Enoch* is important for our understanding of various forms of Judaism in the ancient world. There was no "Bible" back then, so we should not impose later canonical ideas on ancient texts in determining their relative importance. *1 Enoch* has its own merit, derived not just from its ancestral relationship with the canonical book of Revelation.

As to its bizarre apocalyptic trappings, this literature is, at its heart, quite simple. *1 Enoch* squirms beneath the same basic religious questions we still ask today: Where does evil come from? Why does God let this happen? What is going to happen in the future? Are the bad people going to be punished? This literature wants to describe the nature of suffering and to convince its hearers that God controls the universe. Good will be rewarded and evil will be punished, but not until the time appointed at the end of history, an end which is coming very soon. *1 Enoch* employs theology, mythology, and imagery to resist those causing suffering and evil.[1]

Creation infuses *1 Enoch* as one the book's primary modes of resistance. Angelic guides repeatedly lead Enoch on tours of the heavens to see the intricate workings of the universe. A section known as the "Astronomical Book" (chaps. 72–82) discusses and calculates the movements of the sun, moon, and stars. Chapters 83–90 contain a section known as the "Animal Apocalypse" in which the entire history of Israel is retold using animals instead of humans. The final section, called the Epistle of Enoch (chaps. 92–105), offers the sea as a repeated metaphor. The created order thus provides a wide array of metaphors and images to the authors of *1 Enoch*; it is indispensable to their worldview.

---

1. The problem of evil was likely not the catalyst for all apocalyptic literature, contra Paulo Sacchi, *Jewish Apocalyptic and its History*, JSJSup 20, trans. W. Short (Sheffield: JSOT Press, 1990), who claimed that the problem of evil was generative for the entire ancient Jewish apocalyptic tradition. See the more nuanced explanation of the growth of the tradition in John J. Collins, *The Apocalyptic Imagination: An Introduction to Jewish Apocalyptic Literature* (Grand Rapids, MI: Eerdmans, 1998).

II. Book of Watchers:
A Worldview Animated by Creation

1 Enoch is an anthology of apocalyptic literature, written across several centuries during the Hellenistic and later time periods. The first section, called the Book of Watchers (chaprs. 1–36), is also one of its oldest and will be the main focus of this chapter. The Book of Watchers turns repeatedly to images of mountains, rivers, waterfalls, valleys, animals, and birds. Mountains and high places melt like wax before a candle (*1 Enoch* 1:6). Giants maraud the earth, consuming all the produce and sinning against birds, beasts, reptiles, and fish (*1 Enoch* 7:5). The book's final chapters (21–26) fetishize forests. From beginning to end, creation animates its worldview.

The opening paragraphs of the Book of Watchers repeatedly call for the observation and contemplation of creation:

- "Contemplate all (his) works, and observe the works of heaven, how they do not alter their paths. . ."[2] (2:1 Hermeneia)

- "Observe the signs of summer. . ." (4:1 Hermeneia)

- "Contemplate all the trees; their leaves blossom green on them, and they cover the trees. . ." (5:1 Hermeneia)

- "Contemplate all these works, and understand that he who lives for all the ages made all these works. . ." (5:2 Hermeneia)

According to the Book of Watchers, observation and contemplation ought to lead to the proper lesson: that God controls the universe and that everything works properly: "His work proceeds and pro-

---

2. The textual history of *1 Enoch* is quite complicated. Our earliest full copies of it are in a language called Ethiopic. We also have earlier fragmentary pieces of it in Greek and Aramaic (from the Dead Sea Scrolls). There are two main sources for an English translation. First, *The Old Testament Pseudepigrapha* (OTP), ed. James H. Charlesworth, 2 vols. (Garden City, NY: Doubleday, 1983) and George W. E. Nickelsburg and James C. VanderKam, *1 Enoch: A New Translation Based on the Hermeneia Commentary* (Minneapolis: Fortress Press, 2004). I will alternate between these two translations, noted as either "Hermeneia" or "OTP."

gresses from year to year. And all his work prospers and obeys him, and it does not change; but everything functions in the way in which God has ordered it" (5:2 OTP).

What would compel an author to write such things? Was there really any question at this point in Jewish history whether God was an omnipotent creator? Somewhere behind this text must lay an experience to the contrary—some piece of propaganda that contradicted these statements. If not, there would be no reason for the author to write them. If you were to stand outside my house on a random Tuesday evening, you might hear me say repeatedly: "Stop hitting your brother." From such a statement you could rightly imply that someone was hitting his brother. We can use the same logic here: starting an apocalyptic text with statements of God's omnipotence and the regularity of creation suggests that:

1. The authors and the community were experiencing a challenge to God's omnipotence, and

2. The created order was involved in that challenge to God's omnipotence.

As we will see below, the authors of the Book of Watchers were experiencing just these very things. The hegemony of kingship in the Hellenistic period and the environmental impacts of its warfare form a crisp backdrop against which we can understand the Book of Watchers' emphases. The authors' belief in God as creator and the importance of creation comprise the standard against which they judge the era in which they lived.[3] We turn now to a detailed exploration of that era in which the Book of Watchers was written, which will help explain its language about God and creation.

---

3. See H. H. Schmid, "Creation, Righteousness, and Salvation: 'Creation Theology' as the Broad Horizon of Biblical Theology," in *Old Testament Theology*, ed. Bernhard Anderson (Minneapolis: Fortress Press, 1985), 102–17.

III. Introducing the Elephant Kings[4]

Alexander the Great did not leave a clear plan of succession before his death. Having conquered from Greece to Egypt to India, after his death this vast territory was divided among his generals, the Diadochoi (which means "the Successors"). Like a group of siblings who squabble over their parents' inheritance, these successors fought almost constantly over their territory. The Diadochoi, and those who followed them, were "hyper imperialists" with grandiose agendas.[5] In eras before them, kings tied their reigns to a bloodline and a specific territory. For example, Philip, Alexander's father, was "King of Macedonia." Those kings that followed Alexander, however, had no historical or geographical claim to their territories. This "intentional vagueness" meant that they could be kings of "whichever land they could conquer."[6]

These men made themselves kings through war and conquest. During the Hellenistic period, armies bloated, battlefields expanded, and the impact on local populations multiplied. War was so pervasive that it is a wonder that ancient people wrote about it at all, "so familiar must every person have been with the composition of armies, arms, soldiers and soldiering, and the impact of conflict on the civilian landscape."[7]

The Hellenistic kings buttressed their war making with coordinated propaganda. We can get fascinating access to this propaganda by looking at the coins they stamped in their kingdoms. In the initial decades after Alexander, the Diadochoi placed Alexander's head on their coins. This *imitatio alexandri*[8] sought to ape Alexander's power, prestige, and success. Seleucis I (312–281 BCE), for instance, used Alexander's head almost exclusively. The reverse sides of his coins often included Dionysus, an attempt to recall that god's mythic

4. Paul J. Kosmin, *The Land of the Elephant Kings: Space, Territory, and Ideology in the Seleucid Empire* (Cambridge, MA: Harvard University Press, 2014).

5. John Serrati, "The Hellenistic World at War: Stagnation or Development?" in *Oxford Handbook of Warfare in the Classical World*, ed. Brian Campbell and Lawrence A. Tritle (Oxford: Oxford University Press, 2013), 179.

6. Angelos Chaniotis, *War in the Hellenistic World: A Social and Cultural History* (Oxford: Wiley-Blackwell), 57.

7. Serrati, "Hellenistic World at War," 179.

8. This phrase, which means "imitation of Alexander," is from Chaniotis, *War in the Hellenistic World*, 58.

conquest of the east and legitimize Alexander and Seleucis as the god's inheritors.[9] Seleucis also claimed that the god Apollo was his ancestor, establishing a cult in his honor in Syria. To reinforce this tinge of deity, many coins show Apollo sitting with a bow. Seleucis I's coins also depict several types of animals, most prominently elephants, bulls, and horses. The elephants often pull a chariot driven by Athena. Elephants never pulled chariots in battle, so these images are best understood as propaganda and projections of power, not literal depictions of war tactics.

Ancient Greek coins in the Altes Museum Berlin. Image by Sailko. Courtesy of Wikimedia Commons. Top: Alexander's horse, Boucephalus, and an elephant represent power and divinity for Seleucis the king. Below: King Antiochus depicted as the God Apollo.

9. See the discussion of Dionysus's legacy in Diodorus Siculus, *Library of History*, trans. C. H. Oldfather, Loeb Classical Library No. 303 (Cambridge, MA: Harvard University Press, 1935), 3.65. See also Arthur Houghton and Catherine Lorber, eds., *Seleucid Coins, a Comprehensive Catalogue, Part 1: Seleucis I–Antiochus III* (Lancaster, PA: American Numismatic Society, 2003), 1:6.

Antiochus I Soter "Savior" (294–261 BCE) follows Seleucis I as leader of the Seleucid kingdom. His "most significant iconographic innovation" was to introduce non-Alexander portraits to the precious metal coinage, a maneuver followed by almost all of his successors.[10] Antiochus also needed to commemorate the now dead but divine Seleucis I. He did this by introducing horns to the ruler's head. We might look, for example, at a silver tetradrachm struck at Sardes, where Antiochus's court was located from 276 to 274.[11] On the front (called the obverse by numismatists), it shows the head of Seleucis I with horns. On the reverse we find ΒΑΣΙΛΕΩΣ ΑΝΤΙΟΧΟΥ (Antiochus the King) with a horned horse head.[12] These horns originate in a legend told about Seleucis I, in which he wrestles and subdues a wild bull at one of Alexander's sacrifices. The horns symbolize divinity.

The details in these coins show their propagandistic importance. They breathe myth, ritual, violence, and divinity into the king and vivify an empire that engulfs the whole environment, both animals and humans. A hymn of praise, called an encomium, to Ptolemy II (the Ptolemies, based in Egypt, were the main rivals of the Seleucids) narrates the kind of ideology their kingship projected:

> "All of the sea, the earth and the rushing rivers acknowledge Ptolemy; around flows a crowd of cavalry and a crowd of infantry equipped with flashing bronze. In wealth he outweighs all other kings; so much wealth flows into his household each day from everywhere. His people go about their tasks in security; for no one dares to cross the Nile fertile in monsters, no one who comes by land raises the cry of war in foreign villages; nor has any swift ship from the sea, girded for war, surged forward to pillage Egypt's cattle. So powerful is the man established on these broad plains, blond Ptolemy who knows how to shake the spear of war and who as a good king guards what he has inherited and himself adds to it."[13]

10. Houghton and Lorber, *Seleucid Coins,* 1:115.

11. Ibid., 1:123.

12. Ibid., 2: plate 18, coin number 322. For a description see 1:124.

13. Michael M. Sage, *Warfare in Ancient Greece: A Sourcebook* (London: Routledge, 1996), 201.

This "royal-military ideology"[14] depicts a king who rules not just human beings, but all of creation. The elephant kings and their propaganda challenged the tenets of the Jewish belief in their God's omnipotence and sovereignty. In the Book of Watchers, we can see the way the book militates against the ideology of the elephant kings. God is in control and will come with "ten million of the holy ones in order to execute judgment upon all," at which point he will "destroy the wicked ones" (*1 Enoch* 1:9 OTP). Enoch's tours of the heavens (chaps. 14–36) testify to God's omnipotence; God is the one who controls the wind, rain, and hail. Enoch is given a message from God to send to the watchers, that they will have no peace (16:3). Enoch's tours are geographically expansive. He sees "all the rivers of the earth" (17:8 OTP), suggesting that God's territory is not divided and offering a riposte to the type of ideology seen in the encomium to Ptolemy, who claimed that all the rivers and the seas acknowledge him. Scholars have long coordinated *1 Enoch* and the Book of Watchers with "the context of propaganda in Hellenistic antiquity."[15] These authors clearly intended to critique "Hellenistic rulers, their armies, and their ideology of conquest."[16]

The Hellenistic kings did more than just project propaganda. The propaganda was in service to a real agenda of conquest. Their constant warring had drastic impacts on local populations, particularly due to its ecological impact. Below we will explore the devastation of animals, agriculture, and forests, which will help us understand the experience of a Jewish community under the hegemony of the elephant kings and the apocalyptic response we see in the Book of Watchers. We then will be situated to anticipate some implications for our study of Revelation.

14. Anathea Portier-Young, *Apocalypse against Empire: Theologies of Resistance in Early Judaism* (Grand Rapids, MI: Eerdmans, 2011), 53.

15. Loren T. Stuckenbruck, "The Origins of Evil in Jewish Apocalyptic Tradition: The Interpretation of Genesis 6:1-4 in the Second and Third Centuries BCE," in *The Fall of the Angels*, ed. Christoph Auffarth and Loren T. Stuckenbruck (Leiden: Brill, 2004), 98.

16. Portier-Young, *Apocalypse against Empire*, 382.

IV. Hellenistic War and the Environment

Humans in the eastern Mediterranean have been destroying their environment for millennia. Evidence of depleted megafauna and soil erosion appear from the beginning of the Holocene period, 12,000 years ago.[17] Early urbanism and hunting resulted in deforestation.[18] The rise of agriculture led to further deforestation, destruction of habitat, soil erosion, salinization of soil due to irrigation, and other environmental problems.[19] Ancient people in the Mediterranean experienced many things we would consider to be modern ecological concerns. Water pollution, fish depletion, deforestation, disease, air pollution, and overpopulation all impacted ancient peoples at various times. We are well within the bounds of reason, then, to look for experiences of environmental degradation to explain the way the Book of Watchers depicts the environment.

1. ANIMALS

Because of the nature of modern warfare, we may not think about war and its impact on animals. It all started with the ancient Sumerians, whose reliefs show donkeys pulling soldiers into battle. By 1700 BCE horses and chariots had been introduced into Egypt.[20] Dogs were common in battle because they could be trained to attack only the enemy. They often wore spiked collars and armor. Adrienne Mayor's book *Greek Fire, Poison Arrows, and Scorpion Bombs* describes how many animals were weaponized.[21] Alexander's troops in India learned of new types of snakes, whose venom made spears and ar-

---

17. See Charles L. Redman, *Human Impact on Ancient Environments* (Tucson: University of Arizona Press, 1999), and Susanne Kerner, Rachael J. Dann, and Pernille Bangsgaard, *Climate and Ancient Societies* (Copenhagen: Museum Tusculanum Press, 2015).

18. Donald J. Hughes, *Environmental Problems of the Greeks and Romans: Ecology in the Ancient Mediterranean* (Baltimore: Johns Hopkins University Press, 2014), 27–28.

19. Ibid., 28–36.

20. Ibid., 158.

21. Adrienne Mayor, *Greek Fire, Poison Arrows, and Scorpion Bombs: Biological and Chemical Warfare in the Ancient World* (Woodstock, NY: Overlook Duckworth, 2003).

rows even more deadly. Bees or other flying insects could be placed in jars and hurled at opposing armies. Aeneas Tacticus, who wrote a treatise on how to survive siege warfare, suggests releasing stinging insects into tunnels being dug by those laying siege.[22]

The most dramatic animal in Hellenistic warfare is the elephant. The successors to Alexander used elephants from both India and Africa.[23] They were captured, trained, and used in battle, depleting their wild populations.[24] In combat, elephants wore armor and carried a tower from which several soldiers could shoot arrows or throw spears.[25] One ancient historian of the period, Diodorus Siculus, claimed that elephants, because of their size and power, "play a great part in turning the scale to victory."[26] Despite these words, most evidence suggests the contrary: elephants were rarely decisive in major battles. Armies employed them to intimidate. Their role in battle turns out to be quite similar to their role on coins: mostly for psychological impact and propaganda rather than tactical advantage. Elephants could also be detrimental. They were hard to control, often turned to flight, and in such instances could actually damage their own side. Because of this, most elephant drivers carried a spike that could be driven into the elephant's head if it started to rampage against its own troops.[27]

Diodorus discusses a battle pitting Antigonus and his son Demetrius against Seleucis and Ptolemy (who, at this point, were briefly allied with one another).[28] This large battle included cavalry and elephants. Their Indian leaders drove the elephants headlong into battle even though they began to be tormented by their wounds

22. Leslie Whittaker Hunter and S. A. Handford, *Aineiou Poliorketika* (Oxford: Clarendon Press, 1927).

23. See Diodorus Siculus, *Library of History*, 3.36, where he discusses Ptolemy II and his love for hunting elephants. He would reward those who could subdue the greatest and strongest of them.

24. Hughes, *Environmental Problems*, 160.

25. Serrati, "The Hellenistic World at War," 191.

26. Diodorus Siculus, *Library of History*, 2.35.

27. Serrati, "The Hellenistic World at War," 191.

28. Diodorus describes this as a situation in which Seleucis goads Ptolemy into battle for little more than spite and hatred. Ptolemy, he says, was "spurred on by Seleucis because of his hostility toward Antigonus" (19.80-97).

from arrows, spears, or swords. The Seleucids also had a device for countering the elephants' charge, called a κάραξ (*Karax*), which was a spike that was laid on the ground. They were designed so that the elephants would step on them, injuring their feet. In defensive battles, armies could place these in advance in order to protect certain flanks or parts of a city. In this battle, the Seleucids must have had a mobile version that they could set up quickly depending on the enemy's deployment. According to Diodorus, the elephants were "tormented by their wounds" and "began to cause disorder." Later, the Romans so perfected the art of defeating elephants that by the end of the Hellenistic period their use was almost completely abandoned.

Hellenistic kings could certainly not claim: "No animals were harmed in the making of this kingdom." Ethical treatment of animals is a modern concern, so we should not expect to find our own concerns discussed in the ancient context. Nevertheless, animals, and elephants in particular, serve as a clear example of the kind of ecological impact that war had: severe violence, pain, death, and population decline that was imposed upon the animal kingdom.

2. AGRICULTURE

In the ancient world, much like today, those most intimately connected with the land are the most vulnerable to environmental devastation.[29] In the Hellenistic period, these were farmers whose existence depended upon the food they produced. Their survival was fraught on its own, living just at the level of subsistence, barely able to survive. Hellenistic kingship often made survival even more difficult, either through severe taxation or royal seizure of the best properties.[30] War could bring starvation, migration, slavery, or death

29. Robert Mendelsohn, Ariel Dinar, and Larry Williams, "The Distributional Impact of Climate Change on Rich and Poor Countries," *Environment and Development Economics* 2 (2006): 159–78.

30. The Hefzibah inscription indicates that some land was seized by kings and designated for royal use. See Andrea M. Berlin, "Between Large Forces: Palestine in the Hellenistic Period," *Biblical Archeologist* 60, no. 1 (1997): 2–51, here 13–14.

because "the countryside and its economic activities were the greatest victims of wars."[31]

In book seven of his histories, Herodotus describes an advancing Persian army so big that it would drink the rivers dry. Although this is likely an exaggeration, it demonstrates the amount of resources ancient armies consumed to support their soldiers and animals. Alexander, for instance, allotted the seven thousand horses in his cavalry ten pounds of grain and ten gallons of water every day.[32] Theophrastus, an ancient writer who was interested in plants and trees, probably does not exaggerate when he notes that an advancing army could trample fields, completely destroying them. The next year's crop could be endangered as well because of the way the ground was compacted.[33] Troops also lived off the crops of their enemies. During the Hellenistic period, siege warfare became more common, which protracted the time armies were active and multiplied the impact on local agriculture and landscapes. Ancient Latin authors would complain about abandoned fields (*agri deserti*) because untended land could have an impact on soil, water, and food availability.[34]

Theophrastus tells a story about a settlement on the island of Crete that was destroyed by war, leaving the land uncultivated for six years.[35] As a result, the once-plentiful springs and streams in the area stopped providing water. The water returned only after the farmers resumed their work. This story probably alludes to erosion that results when farmers abandoned their terraced agriculture.[36] When the cultivation stopped as a result of war, the local population experienced environmental consequences.[37]

---

31. Chaniotis, *War in the Hellenistic World*, 122.

32. Hughes, *Environmental Problems*, 159.

33. Donald J. Hughes, "Warfare and Environment in the Ancient World," in *Oxford Handbook of Warfare in the Classical World*, ed. Brian Campbell and Lawrence A. Tritle (Oxford: Oxford University Press, 2013), 130.

34. Hughes, *Environmental Problems*, 155.

35. The story survives in Pliny's *Natural History* 31.53 and Seneca's *Natural Inquiries* 3.11.5.

36. Chaniotis, *War in the Hellenistic World*, 127.

37. Modern ecology would see agriculture as the original disruptor of a natural ecosystem. Theophrastus obviously does not see it that way.

Armies also damaged the land on purpose. Cereals and grains comprised about 75 percent of the ancient person's diet and these crops were the easiest for armies to destroy by consumption, trampling, or fire. Plutarch reports that Cleomenes, the King of Sparta in the third century BCE, had soldiers drag planks of wood across fields in order to trample them:

> Cleomenes quickly took his soldiers, marched past the enemy by a different route, and at daybreak appeared suddenly before the city of Argos, ravaging the plain and destroying the grain, not cutting this down, as usual, with sickles and knives, but beating it down with great pieces of wood [ἀλλὰ κόπτων ξύλοις μεγάλοις] fashioned like spear-shafts. These his soldiers plied as if in sport, while passing by, and with no effort at all they would crush and ruin all the crop.[38]

Plutarch mentions this not because of the devastation itself, but because it was done in an unusual way (not the normal sickles and knives). Had they used the normal techniques, it would not have been worth mentioning, because such devastation of the land was a normal part of the experience of war.

Olive trees and grape vines took more effort to destroy, but the impact of their destruction lasted much longer. Grapes take at least two years to begin to produce fruit; olives take at least six years.[39] Livestock was also under threat, as it served as a common source of booty for armies. Maritime warfare could also shut down trade, leading to economic devastation.

The sum total of these occurrences—the impact of war upon the land and people's livelihoods—would often lead to unrest, dissatisfaction, and subsequent conflicts that "threatened social unity."[40] A war in the Argolid discussed by the ancient author Polybius demon-

---

38. Plutarch, *Cleomenes*, in *Plutarch Lives* X, trans. Bernadotte Perrin, Loeb Classical Library (Cambridge, MA: Harvard University Press, 1921), 26.1.

39. Reinder Neef, "Introduction, Development and Environmental Implications of Olive Culture: The Evidence from Jordan," in *Man's Role in the Shaping of the Eastern Mediterranean Landscape*, ed. S. Bottema, G. Entjes-Nieborg, and W. van Zeist (Rotterdam: A. A. Balkema, 1990), 305.

40. Chaniotis, *War in the Hellenistic World*, 129.

strates the psychological impact of the destruction of the landscape. Cleomenes attacked Antigonus's position, which, Polybius says, may have seemed rash at first. But Cleomenes's real goal was not to win, but to ravage the countryside. He knew that if "the country were laid waste up to the walls," the Argives would be "vexed." The Argives do indeed strike out in vexation and anger, while Cleomenes, "having carried out his intention of devastating the country and thus striking terror into the enemy," retired to his own country in safety.[41] This example demonstrates the connection between the fate of a people, an advancing army, and its devastating consequences on the land.

3. TREES AND FORESTS

Visitors to the eastern Mediterranean today revel in the beauty of the hills and their mixture of olives, grapes, and redolent herbs. This landscape, however, results from "massive environmental degradation brought about . . . by the pressure of long-term settlement and growing population."[42] The region was once replete with forests of various types of cedars, pine, and oak. These forests partly explain the growth of civilizations; the history of humans in the Mediterranean region is entwined with trees, which had both a practical and spiritual value. Pliny notes this connection between human origins and trees, particularly their ancient spiritual role: "nor do we pay greater worship to images shining with gold and ivory than to the forests and to the very silences that they contain."[43]

Theophrastus, when discussing that which can harm trees, distinguishes between those things that happen to them spontaneously (αὐτόματα) and the "violent forms" (βίαιος) that are caused by humans when they strike (πληγή).[44] Exploitation of trees was part of all

41. Polybius, *The Histories* I, trans. W. R. Paton, Loeb Classical Library No. 128 (Cambridge, MA: Harvard Unversity Press, 1922), 2.64.

42. Clive Ponting, *A Green History of the World: The Environment and the Collapse of Great Civilizations* (New York: Penguin, 1991), 74.

43. Pliny the Elder, *Natural History* IV, trans. H. Rackham, Loeb Classical Library No. 370 (Cambridge, MA: Harvard University Press, 1945), 12.2.3.

44. Theophrastus, *De Causis Plantarum*, trans. Arthur Hort, Loeb Classical Library, vol. 1 (Cambridge, MA: Harvard University Press, 1916), 5.1.15.

ancient Mediterranean civilizations.[45] Plato articulates the experience of deforestation and its impacts poignantly:

> What now remains compared with what then existed is like the skeleton of a sick man, all the fat and the soft earth having wasted away, and only the bare framework of the land being left . . . there are some mountains which now have nothing but food for bees, but they had trees not very long ago.[46]

Trees played an important role in the spiritual imaginations of the ancient people, who were also aware of the effects of deforestation.

Hellenistic warfare made extensive use of wood. Xenophon calls war a *techne*, a technology for which one needed to know the tools, trades, and tactics for success.[47] An increase in technology and emphasis on new techniques suggest that in the Hellenistic period we see a "revolution in the concrete way of doing war."[48] Siege warfare becomes more common, which we can see through excavations with increased fortification for towns and cities. One ancient author wrote a whole treatise about how to survive a siege.[49] Siege warfare required timber for the creation of catapults and siege works. Alexander's long siege of Tyre provides a concrete example, one that "must have had a significant effect on the timber resources of the neighborhood of Tyre."[50] One Hellenistic king, Demetrius, had the audacity to give himself the nickname "The Besieger." He created a famous siege work, called the *helepolis* (i.e., the "city taker"), that was simply enormous. It had platforms 50 cubits (approximately 75 feet) square and catapults that could throw stones weighing up to 80 kilograms. The

---

45. Sytze Bottema and Henk Woldring, "Anthropogenic Indicators in the Pollen Record of the Eastern Mediterranean," in *Man's Role in the Shaping of the Eastern Mediterranean Landscape*, ed. S. Bottema, G. Entjes-Nieborg, and W. van Zeist (Rotterdam: A. A. Balkema, 1990).

46. Plato, *Critias*, trans. R. G. Bury, Loeb Classical Library No. 234 (Cambridge, MA: Harvard University Press, 1929), 111.b-c.

47. Serafina Cuomo, *Technology and Culture in Greek and Roman Antiquity* (Cambridge: Cambridge University Press, 2007), 60.

48. Ibid., 42.

49. Aeneias' *Polioketika*. See n. 22 above.

50. Russell Meiggs, *Trees and Timber in the Ancient Mediterranean World* (Oxford: Clarendon Press, 1982), 162.

whole structure measured approximately nine stories high so that weapons could be rained down upon the city. Demetrius's *helepolis* was a war machine worthy of his own nickname.[51]

Timber was also important in shipbuilding. The first century after Alexander's death saw more ships in battle in the Mediterranean than in any other century of ancient history.[52] Antigonus, an early Hellenistic ruler, approached the most famous ship builders in the ancient world, the Phoenicians, to help him create a fleet. Polybius reports that:

> [Antigonus] himself collected wood cutters, sawyers, and ship-wrights from all sides, and carried wood to the sea from Lebanon. There were eight thousand men employed in cutting and sawing the timber and one thousand pair of draught animals in transporting it.[53]

Technological and tactical innovations had an impact on the development of how ships were built as well. In previous time periods, ships were built for speed, with the goal of ramming and sinking the enemy's ships. Ships now had missiles and catapults and carried large armies with a goal of disarming and disabling the enemy from a distance. As a result, kings needed larger and larger ships, which would have "increased the demand for timber" from all parts of the Mediterranean.[54]

V. The Book of Watchers Explained

Our exploration of the propaganda of the Hellenistic kings and the devastation brought on by their warring paints a backdrop against which the Book of Watchers' view of God and creation can be better understood. It is impossible to pinpoint exactly when and where this text was written, but most scholars would agree its origins can be found in the early Hellenistic period. The authors of the early

---

51. See Polybius, *The Histories,* 10.91.2-6.
52. Meiggs, *Trees and Timber*, 133.
53. Polybius, *The Histories,* 19.58.
54. Meiggs, *Trees and Timber*, 139.

parts of *1 Enoch* were "parties to conflict and victims of violence, oppression and persecution."[55]

The Jewish historian Josephus, writing in the first century CE, describes the general situation that his people faced during this time:

> As these [i.e., the Diadochoi] quarreled and fought jealously with one another, each for his own kingdom, the result was that continual and prolonged wars arose, and the cities suffered through their struggles and lost many of their inhabitants, so that all of Syria at the hands of Ptolemy, the son of Lagus, who was then called *Soter*, suffered the reverse of that which was indicated by his surname.[56]

The word "*Soter*" in Greek means "savior." Josephus points out the irony in someone who calls himself a savior bringing such destruction and violence into the world. The Book of Watchers itself offers a general assessment of the complaint that is brought before God that comports well with the scenario Josephus described:

> Their groaning has ascended (into heaven) but they could not get out from before the face of the oppression that is being wrought on earth. (*1 Enoch* 9:10 OTP)

The Book of Watchers originated in this experience of war and violence wrought by the early Hellenistic kings. Because of a lack of specific evidence, further precision is impossible. Our comparison here between the Book of Watchers and its context must remain impressionistic. We have learned enough, however, to see how the environmental components of its context were a catalyst for the Book of Watchers' words about God, humanity, and creation.

1. HEAVENLY PHENOMENA AND THEIR DEVIATIONS

My family and I recently stayed up late to watch a lunar eclipse. Meteorologists and astrologers could pinpoint the exact second the

---

55. George W. E. Nickelsburg, *1 Enoch: A Commentary on the Book of 1 Enoch Chapters 1–36, 81–108*, Hermeneia Series (Minneapolis: Fortress Press, 2001), 63.

56. Josephus, *Jewish Antiquities 12–13*, trans. H. St. J. Thackeray and Ralph Marcus, Loeb Classical Library No. 365 (Cambridge, MA: Harvard University Press, 1943), 12.1.3.

eclipse would start. Celestial phenomena run like clockwork—indeed we set our clocks by them. This regularity and predictability is part of the experience of the natural world, often referred to as the laws of nature. The seasons always change. Trees bear fruit at certain times of the year. Observation of such phenomena was essential for the survival of ancient people, telling them when to plant and when to harvest. The Book of Watchers begins by calling for the examination and observation of this regularity. Creation functions as an ordered expression of God's power. In chapter 5, verdant trees and the sea exemplify obedience and consistency:

> Contemplate all the trees; their leaves blossom green on them, and they cover the trees. And all their fruit is for glorious honor. Contemplate all these works, and understand that he who lives for all the ages made these works. And his works take place from year to year, and they all carry out their works for him, and their works do not alter, but they all carry out his word. Observe how, in like manner, the sea and the rivers carry out and do not alter their works from his words. (5:1-4 Hermeneia)

Trees have leaves and bear fruit in the proper season; rivers flow ever on; the sea does not part. Such regularity contrasts with those who have not done the commandments of the Lord:

> But as for you, you have not been long-suffering and you have not done the commandments of the Lord, but you have transgressed and spoken slanderously grave and harsh words with your impure mouths against his greatness . . . Therefore, you shall curse your days. (5:4-5 OTP)

The disobedient unrighteous clash against a background marked by regularity and obedience.

Later parts of the Book of Watchers recapitulate this theme, but the imagery changes from pastoral to cosmic. In chapter 18, Enoch is shown the origin of the winds and how God has "embroidered all creation as well as the foundations of the earth" (18:1-2 OTP). Enoch is then shown a "desolate and terrible place," with no heaven above, no earth below, not even water or birds (18:12 OTP). This terrible place is the "prison house" for the stars, the ones that "have transgressed the commandments of God from the beginning of their rising because they did not arrive punctually" (18:15 OTP). In this example, the sin of the watchers is projected upon the cosmos, likened to stars that no longer arrive on time. Because they deviate, a special place of torment is reserved for their punishment.

Today we do not think that stars have a choice in what they do; the moon does not start an eclipse when it feels like it. Yet, this is the very scenario that the Book of Watchers suggests. It presents elements of the environment and cosmos—trees, oceans, and stars—as if they had independent personalities.[57] Observable reality becomes a "cosmic parable" that exhorts its reader to draw the appropriate implication.[58] The created order is an "exemplar of regularity and faithfulness" that allows the basis for judging those that deviate.[59] We often today think of sin as something personal, involving ourselves and those most intimately around us. The Book of Watchers suggests a larger scope for sin. Sin is more cosmic than personal. It is the dark matter of the universe. Evil and violence have so thoroughly infiltrated the structures of the world that it feels as if the sea has left its boundaries and the sun, moon, and stars no longer follow predictable patterns.

This theological vision offered by the Book of Watchers has significant ecological implications that can help us today. Our mind-set today emerges from a long history of western thought, one that has tended to separate the human from nature. The Book of Watchers offers no whiff of this whatsoever. The drama of sin and evil plays out on a cosmic scale. In its context of Hellenistic propaganda, with its kings and their grandiose claims to divinity and ultimate control, the Book of Watchers sees that the whole of creation is at stake.

---

57. See Michael E. Stone, "The Parabolic Use of Natural Order in Judaism of the Second Temple Age," in *Gilgul: Essays on Transformation, Revolution, and Permanence in the History of Religions*, ed. S. Shaked, Philippe Gignoux, D. Shulman, and G. G. Stroumsa (Leiden: Brill, 1987), 298–308.

58. Randal A. Argall, *1 Enoch and Sirach: A Comparative Literary and Conceptual Analysis of the Themes of Revelation, Creation and Judgment* (Atlanta: Scholars Press, 1995), 101.

59. Stone, "Parabolic Use of Natural Order," 300–301.

2. THE SIN OF THE WATCHERS AND THE VOICE OF THE EARTH

1 Enoch chapters 6–11 tells the myth of the watchers who rebel from heaven, swear an oath together, and descend and impregnate the beautiful women on the earth. These angels teach illicit things to the women. The women become pregnant and give birth to giants. These giants "were devouring the labor [or produce] of all the sons of men, and men were not able to supply them" (7:3 OTP). Insatiable in their gluttony, the giants turn on the people and "sin against" birds, wild beasts, creeping things, and fish (7:5). They devour the very list of things (plus fish) that Noah brought on the ark in Genesis 6. Still not full, they turn on one another and eventually "drink the blood," which for a Jew was "the ultimate abomination and violation of created life" (see Gen 9:5-6).[60] This mythic description of the sins of the watchers comports well with local populations' experience of warfare in the Hellenistic period. Devastated crops, billeting armies, and exploited livestock—in sum, ill treatment of flora and fauna—pulse in the background of the Book of Watchers' mythology.

The way *1 Enoch* tells this myth about the watchers is remarkably earth-centric. After describing the destruction brought by the watchers and their giant offspring, the first voice is given to the earth itself: "And then the earth brought an accusation against the oppressors" (7:6 OTP). The good angels, Michael, Sariel, Raphael, and Gabriel observed carefully (9:1) the terrible things that were happening, and they credit the earth with giving voice to the suffering:

> They [i.e., the angels] said to one another: "The earth, devoid (of inhabitants), raises the voice of their cries to the gates of heaven."
> (9:2 Hermeneia)

The watchers' appetite devours creation itself, and once devoid of life, the earth itself rises to the challenge and cries out. The Book of Watchers understands damage to the land as a sin against creation itself. This becomes a subset of the text's broader critique of empire—that the ambitions of the self-made kings were not just causing

---

60. Nickelsburg, *1 Enoch*, 186.

bloodshed upon the earth, but were disrupting the very way the earth itself was supposed to work, an affront to creation.

While one might read the devastation wrought to the earth and its creatures in *1 Enoch* 6-11 and revolt, finding it an offensive scene of destruction, we must remember its context. The depiction of the watchers and their devastation does not *prescribe* an ideology that destroys the earth, but instead *describes* the experiences of a suffering community during a period of protracted and repetitive war. What image could better capture the experience of the Diadochoi, the elephant kings, than giants who maraud the earth, its produce, and its animals?

3. FIXATION ON FORESTS

Trees infuse the final eleven chapters of the Book of Watchers. In chapters 24 and 25 one particular tree and its scent transfix Enoch. The angel Michael explains that this tree is reserved for the end, when it will provide fruit for the righteous and pious (25:5). In 26:1 Enoch sees a blessed place shaded with branches from trees previously cut, new growth coming from dead branches. Chapter 27 describes a vision of a "blessed land, entirely filled with trees," in the midst of which is an accursed valley reserved for the wicked who will undergo judgment. In chapter 28 a series of solitary wildernesses are full of trees, producing nuts, fragrances, and seeds. Chapter 29 speaks of a tree of judgment. Chapters 30 and 31 discuss beautiful trees, with good fruit and pleasant odor. Chapter 32 discusses the most famous tree from the Hebrew tradition, that of the knowledge of good and evil, which caused Enoch's ancestors to be expelled from the garden.

In the final chapters of the Book of Watchers, trees populate those places reserved for the elect and righteous. The vision in chapter 26 serves as an example:

> And from there I proceeded to the center of the earth, and I saw a blessed place where there were trees that had branches that abide and sprout. And there I saw a holy mountain. (26:1-2 Hermeneia)

The vision continues with more mountains and valleys that were deep and made of hard rock, where no trees grew. The presence of trees (or lack thereof) distinguishes that land which is "blessed" from that which is "cursed" (see 27:1). This vision has a deep impact on Enoch: "And I marveled at the mountain, and I marveled at the valley, I marveled exceedingly" (26:6 Hermeneia).

The Book of Watchers' use of trees should be seen initially as an extended meditation on the tree of the knowledge of good and evil from the book of Genesis. By envisioning this tree at the end of time, the text suggests that the *endzeit* (the last days) will become like the *urzeit* (the first days). Given what we know about timber exploitation and the importance of trees in people's theological imaginations, we also ought to see an environmental perspective in these chapters. It is no accident that the places of torment in the Book of Watchers are those devoid of trees. If a group is experiencing a dearth of trees—no silence of the forest, no large specimens at which to marvel (see Ezekiel 31:3b), or no wood to build fire or home—they see themselves as impoverished by those forces eliminating such possibilities. The Book of Watchers counters this experience with myriad individual trees, wonderful in smell and appearance, and a vision of the end times marked by wild, vast forests. Their return, importance, and persistence are an environmental critique of the experience of Hellenistic empire and its ecological effects—offering a vision of a providential future in which God will restore those essential things that the empires had taken away.

VI. The Book of Watchers' "Ecological Alternative"

Apocalyptic literature, because of its wild visions and crazy scenarios, has often been thought to be a way of disengaging from reality, marked by an emphasis on the ineffable and spiritual. These authors, the argument goes, try to escape the world by pulling back and hoping that God will come and fix everything. Nothing could be farther from the truth. Anathea Portier-Young has argued convincingly that apocalyptic literature is not a "flight from reality." On the contrary, this literature intends to look at the devastation the Jewish people were facing and engage it "head on" by offering a theological and ideological alternative.[61] Because of our explorations of this literature

61. Portier-Young, *Apocalypse against Empire*, xxii.

and its context we can add that the Book of Watchers was also offering an "ecological alternative."

This ecological alternative attests first and foremost that the God
of Israel is sovereign, the one who created and controls the universe.
The self-made elephant kings, who grasp for control and divinity,
are described in the Book of Watchers as a disruption in the very
workings of the cosmos. While this temporarily throws a wrench
into things, the wicked will get their recompense; God's control is
not ultimately in doubt.

Second, the ecological alternative suggests that the earth matters,
that it has a voice. Capricious consumption of produce and destruction of the land—told in the guise of the gluttonous giants—is an
attack on creation itself. The earth's voice rouses God and the good
angels, who write "all sin" (10:8) upon the evil angels that rebelled
from heaven.

Finally, the ecological alternative offers wild and uncultivated
places as the future that God will create. We might call this an environmental critique of Hellenistic empire and its wasteful creation of
"civilization." Enoch sees the vast forests and wildernesses and mar-
vels deeply, perhaps because of their beauty, or perhaps because he
does not know what comes next. Such a future will rely not on human
ingenuity and technology, but on God's providence and continued
role as creator. Because the book's perspective is rooted in God's
role as creator, all things are then in the community of that creation.
As Aldo Leopold says (as quoted at the start of this chapter), one of
the main reasons for our ecological emergency is that we see land as
something to be owned, not something that is part of a community.[62]
The Book of Watchers helps us envision a different way of being.

VII. Revelation's Ancestors Considered

Revelation has many ancestors. John inherited the Jewish Scriptures,
parts of the New Testament, early Christian oral traditions, nonbiblical literature, and religious practices, rituals, and experiences. Rather

---

62. Aldo Leopold, *A Sand County Almanac* (New York: Ballantine Books,
1970), xviii–xix.

than try to discuss broadly and superficially all of the influences on John, I have presented here one very specific example from *1 Enoch* and the Book of Watchers. There are several points of contact between the Book of Watchers and Revelation that we should consider.

1. CREATION INFUSES APOCALYPTIC LITERATURE

As we have seen in *1 Enoch*, creation infuses apocalyptic literature. Were we to spend time looking at other examples, such as parts of the book of Daniel, the Dead Sea Scrolls, the Sibylline Oracles, or *4 Ezra*, the same would hold true, albeit in their own unique ways. Creation theology is the broad horizon of apocalyptic theology.[63] *1 Enoch* seems incapable of expressing its theology without the language of creation. Its understanding of evil is cast as a rupture of creation itself.

The same holds true in Revelation. Creation and the natural world are an integral part of how John formulates his theological point of view. The opening vision in Revelation chapter 4 includes images of a rainbow, precious stone, lightning, and thunder (4:3-5). Living creatures fly around the throne, the first to give praise to God (4:8-9). In the next chapter, praise is given to the lamb by "every creature in heaven and on earth and under the earth and in the sea, and all that is in them" (5:13). At the end of the book, God creates anew (21:1-8). The natural world provides metaphors and images that emphasize God's power as the creator. Such emphases arise naturally in a context in which humans usurp God's role as the one who controls the universe. In the Hellenistic context, Alexander's successors made grandiose claims to sovereignty. A few centuries later John will experience similar propaganda from Rome and its emperors. In such a context, assertions of God's sovereignty and creative power become a subversive, politically dangerous path.

2. EARTH'S ACTIVE ROLE

Creation is not only integral but at times has a voice and its own role to play. Creation does not stand idle in all apocalyptic scenarios.

---

63. This is to paraphrase Schmid, "Creation, Righteousness, and Salvation," 102.

We discussed above the voice that the Book of Watchers gives to the earth itself, calling out for justice. Revelation 12 also personifies the earth, giving it an active role:

> So when the dragon saw that he had been thrown down to the earth, he pursued the woman who had given birth to the male child. But the woman was given the two wings of the great eagle, so that she could fly from the serpent into the wilderness, to her place where she is nourished for a time, and times, and half a time. Then from his mouth the serpent poured water like a river after the woman, to sweep her away with the flood. But the earth came to the help of the woman; it opened its mouth and swallowed the river that the dragon had poured from his mouth. (Rev 12:13-16)

Both the Book of Watchers and Revelation personify the earth in their drama of sin and evil—it is given a direct role to play. We cannot be sure whether the Book of Watchers directly influenced Revelation. Whether John directly borrowed from the Book of Watchers or not is less interesting than asking why they each personified the earth in this way. The authors of both texts understand the integral role the earth plays in an understanding of sin and evil. Sin's domain is not limited to the human sphere. Its tentacles infiltrate the earth itself. This suggests that the stark moral categories of sin and evil are appropriate when talking about treatment of the earth. An apocalyptic ecology will understand that our treatment of the environment has moral importance. To adapt a phrase from Jesus, even the stones are crying out for environmental justice (Luke 19:40).

3. APOCALYPTIC WORLDVIEWS FORGED IN A CONTEXT

Our exploration of the Book of Watchers as one of Revelation's ancestors allows us to see how its apocalyptic point of view is forged in a context. The Book of Watchers is resistance literature, written to counter an empire-seeking ideology. The claims of Hellenistic kings and their warring destruction spurred and shaped the apocalyptic response. The book of Revelation arises in a very similar situation. John's Apocalypse was written at a point in the Roman Empire in which the emperor was making grandiose claims of power and control. The propaganda put forward claimed rule of the sun, moon, stars, earth, and sea. Such claims to control were an affront to John's community and what they believed about their God. Both the Book of Watchers and Revelation offer a clash of kingdoms—the kingdoms of this world are incompatible with God's kingdom.

4. CONTRASTING ESCHATOLOGIES: WILDERNESS OR URBAN?

While our first three points have shown commonality between the Book of Watchers and Revelation, we will end with a contrast. As described above, the vision of the future—the eschatology—in the Book of Watchers is decidedly wild and uncultivated. It shows little hint of civilization or of human beings at all. This offers quite a contrast to the eschatology in Revelation, which depicts an urban future. An enormous city, the new Jerusalem, descends to the earth (21:10). Unlike the many trees in the Book of Watchers, John's new Jerusalem has only one tree, the tree of life, which heals and feeds all the nations (22:2).

The specifics of these two eschatologies may be different, but I suspect they were instigated by similar situations and share some similar assumptions. The authors of both texts were challenged by the status quo. The authors offer something completely different from the reality in which they lived. In the Book of Watchers, the environmental destruction was countered by a wild future untouched by human civilization. In Revelation, the new Jerusalem outdoes the opulence of Rome by a staggering degree—a city built entirely with precious stones and metals. The new creation in Revelation also has no sea, undermining the economy of exploitation and greed from the Roman context. Both texts, in their unique ways, employ environmental components in their invective against the societies in which they lived. Although the details differ, they both offer an ecological alternative to the times in which they lived.

In the end, the Book of Watchers and Revelation describe a world, created by God, that has value and voice. Creation is not merely given to humanity to use; human perspectives do not define creation's importance. On the contrary, the mechanisms of human self-ambition, in all their manifestations, are rejected because of their drastically negative consequences for that creation. We see here what we might call incipient theological environmentalism. If we were to take seriously God's sovereignty as creator and heed the critiques of the devastation wrought by war and empire, the Book of Watchers might offer ways for evaluating our own ecological crises today. An apocalyptic ecology might find a beneficial starting point in the final words from the Book of Watchers:

> And when I saw, I blessed—and I shall always bless—the Lord of glory, who has wrought great and glorious wonders, to show his great deeds to his angels and to the spirits of human beings, so that they might see the work of his might and glorify the deeds of his hands and bless him forever. (36:4 Hermeneia)

CHAPTER THREE

Revelation's Upbringing

Critique of Empire and Its Ecological Components

"Announcing your plans is a good way to hear God laugh."
—Al Swearengen (Deadwood)

Dr. Martin Luther King Jr. grew up in an age that shaped how he saw the world. A nation rampant with racist segregation and Jim Crow laws had barely moved beyond its roots of slavery. Had King been raised in a different part of the world, or even a different part of the country, his way of viewing the world may have been different. He was born, however, in the southern United States (Atlanta, 1929) and raised in a context of overt racism and structural sin. King was a prophet in the biblical sense—someone whose context and upbringing caused him to see how structures of injustice are inimical to the aims of God.

King wasn't the first to see segregation as an evil form of racism, but he did have a unique insight into its persistence. His father was a vocal critic of segregation and an important figure in Atlanta's black community.[1] His schools were segregated. He could not use public

---

1. James H. Cone, *Martin & Malcolm & America: A Dream or a Nightmare?* (Maryknoll, NY: Orbis Books, 2001), 22.

parks and swimming pools while most whites looked the other way. His initial instinct was to hate white people: "How can I love a race of people who hate me?"[2] His experiences profiled the problem, but also laid the groundwork for his prescription. King's message was framed by love and optimism, a fact that he attributed specifically to his upbringing:

> It is quite easy for me to think of a God of love mainly because I grew up in a family where love was central . . . It is quite easy for me to think of the universe as basically friendly mainly because of my uplifting hereditary and environmental circumstances . . . It is impossible to get at the roots of one's religious attitudes without taking into account the psychological and historical factors that play upon the individual.[3]

King's upbringing, the context in which he was raised and formed, helped him to come to this realization and shaped his opinions and his actions.

The same could be said of John of Patmos. Although we know few specifics about his life, he was raised and formed in a context as well, and the nature of that context shaped his ministry and message. In John's context, the problem was not segregation, but the Roman Empire's claim to control the universe. Such claims were an affront to John's beliefs, and he instigates a battle of imaginations for who truly controls the universe. This chapter will argue that the cosmic propaganda and environmental situation of the Roman Empire comprised a significant part of John's experience and shaped his critique of Rome's claims to power and control.

I. Cosmic Propaganda in the Roman Empire

Around 9 BCE the provincial council in Roman Asia held a competition to see who could come up with the best way to honor Caesar Augustus. The winners proposed reorganizing the calendar around Augustus's birthday. September 23 became the new beginning of

---

2. As quoted in ibid., 23.
3. As quoted in ibid., 19.

the year as well as the date when provincial officers would begin their yearly duties. Augustus was imprinting imperial order, giving the old world a "fresh start, a new origin."[4] The decree announcing this change said some lofty things about Caesar Augustus:

> Providence that ordains our whole life has established with zeal and distinction that which is most perfect in our life by bringing Augustus, whom she filled with virtue as a benefaction to all humanity; sending to us and to those after us a savior who put an end to war and brought order to all things.[5]

Augustus saves humanity, ends war, and rules time itself. These words about Augustus introduce the depth and the breadth of the propaganda that accompanied Rome's domination and its rulers. In the first part of this chapter we will explore some of the details of this propaganda and how it formed the context that spurred John's apocalypse.

1. CALLING THE EMPEROR A GOD

In a culture like that of the modern-day United States, which purports a separation between church and state, it can be very difficult for us to wrap our heads around the varieties of Greco-Roman religion. In the ancient world, religion and politics were inseparable. Cities paid for temples and claimed the protection of deities. In Ephesus, for example, the goddess Artemis was supreme. Her role in Ephesus was known around the ancient world, as was the size and beauty of her temple there. She was called "lord," "savior," and a "heavenly goddess."[6] In an inscription from 44 CE, her temple was called the "adornment of the whole province."[7] The patronage of Artemis cut across all sectors of society in ancient Ephesus: children were dedicated to her and economic structures ran through her cult (see Acts 19). Her temple provided refuge and housed precious items

---

4. Steven J. Friesen, *Imperial Cults and the Apocalypse of John: Reading Revelation in the Ruins* (Oxford: Oxford University Press, 2001), 33.

5. As quoted in ibid., 12.

6. Paul R. Trebilco, *The Early Christians in Ephesus from Paul to Ignatius* (Tübingen: Mohr Siebeck, 2004), 22.

7. Ibid., 20.

and wealth. The whole city celebrated her key festivals. In short: religion, politics, and economics were all mixed together.

Even more removed from our modern forms of religion was an ancient practice in which human rulers would be elevated to the status of a god. In the time when Revelation was written (the final decades of the first century CE), the emperor cult—a form of ancient religion that worshipped Roman emperors as gods—was a vibrant, essential part of the religious landscape of Asia Minor and posted a significant challenge to John and the communities to which he wrote.

Although the emperor cult has roots in earlier traditions (recall the deification of Seleucid kings we discussed in chapter two), we will begin with Caesar Augustus, who ruled from approximately 27 BCE until his death in 14 CE. Born with the name Gaius Octavius, he assumed the name "Augustus" (*Sebastos* in Greek), which means "venerable" or "reverend." This name was "redolent with religious associations."[8] By taking such a name, Augustus opens a path for his subjects to venerate him. Within a few years, temples and shrines were erected on behalf of the emperor and sacrifices and festivals were held in honor of him (and, later, his family). The emperor cult was not imposed on local communities, but the way Augustus practiced his rule invited such worship. Nicolas of Damascus, who wrote a (now fragmentary) life of Caesar Augustus, says: "Because men call him by this name as a mark of esteem for his honour, they revere him with temples and sacrifices, organized by islands and continents, and as cities and provinces they match the greatness of his virtue and the scale of his benefactions towards them."[9]

Local communities would usually ask for permission to establish a cult of the emperor. One of the first was in the city of Pergamum in 29 BCE, which established a cult in honor of Augustus after he won a major military victory over Mark Antony. In 23 CE, emperor Tiberius granted another, this one in the city of Smyrna. Domitian granted one to Ephesus around 90 CE.[10] The cult of the emperor

8. Stephen Mitchell, *Anatolia: Land, Men, and Gods in Asia Minor*, vol. 1, *The Celts and the Impact of Roman Rule* (Oxford: Clarendon Press, 1993), 100.

9. As quoted in ibid., 100.

10. Ephesus built a large temple complex to the emperor and named itself "*neokoros.*" This word *neokoros* was a title normally used of individuals who were priests or wardens of a particular temple. Ephesus started referring to itself as

in Ephesus quickly reached parity with worship of Artemis, demonstrating its infiltration into the religious landscape of Asia Minor by the end of the first century. The iterations of the emperor cult were local, and as its popularity grew, local communities started to compete to see who could best honor the emperor. They "elbowed for position."[11] It is no accident that John's apocalypse shows up at the very same time as the rapid expansion of the emperor cult in the cities in Roman Asia. John was combatting a "serious, and growing, phenomenon"[12] that challenged the early Christians' belief in one God and that God's sovereignty.

2. THE EMPEROR CULT IN APHRODISIAS

One of the most commonly studied examples of the emperor cult in the context of the book of Revelation is a temple complex in ancient Aphrodisias, a close neighbor of the cities John addressed. It became clear early in excavations that a large temple was dedicated to the "gods Sebastoi" (θεοῖς Σεβαστοῖς), in other words, to Augustus and his descendants.[13] This "Sebasteion" (as scholars refer to it) was built with a careful plan. The entrance had a large, ornamental gate (called a "propylon"). Inside was a paved courtyard with a three-story portico (a roofed structure supported by columns) on the left and right. On the ground level, the portico covered small individual rooms, but there was no hallway between them, and on the upper level the rooms were probably completely unused.[14] At the far end of the complex was the temple, dedicated to the emperor(s).

"twice neokoros," by which they meant they oversaw the cult of Artemis and the *Sebastoi* (the emperor and his family). See Steven J. Friesen, *Twice Neokoros: Ephesus, Asia, and the Cult of the Flavian Imperial Family* (Leiden: Brill, 1993).

11. Steven J. Friesen, "The Cult of the Roman Emperors in Ephesos: Temple Wardens, City Titles, and the Interpretation of the Revelation of John," in *Ephesos Metropolis of Asia: An Interdisciplinary Approach to its Archaeology, Religion, and Culture*, ed. Helmut Koester, 229–50 (Valley Forge, PA: Trinity Press International, 2005), 244.

12. Friesen, "Cult of the Roman Emperors," 249.

13. Friesen, *Imperial Cults*, 81.

14. Ibid., 83.

Sketch of Sebasteion porticoes restored from R. R. R. Smith, "The Imperial Reliefs from the Sebasteion at Aphrodisias," *The Journal of Roman Studies* 77 (1987): 88–138, at 94. Used by permission of Cambridge University Press.

The Sebasteion at Aphrodisias was a large, unique, and innovative complex, paid for by a local rich family. More important for our present purposes, however, are the statues that adorned the porticos on the left and right. There is little evidence that the rooms in the porticos were used on a regular basis—the function of this structure was only for public display. The third floor of the north side portico had allegorical statues representing "Day" and "Ocean" and probably "Night" and "Earth."[15] The second story had representations of ethnic groups, islands, and geographical areas that Augustus had conquered. The propaganda here is not hard to discern: Augustus had subdued the earth and its peoples and "such a world was brought into existence by the work of the gods and the conquests of Augustus."[16]

On the south side porticos, the leaders of the Augustan dynasty are depicted as Olympian gods in scenes of conquest. Augustus himself figured prominently in these scenes. For instance, in one scene Augustus is shown naked along with a *nike* (victory) figure and a military trophy. At the bottom is a bound barbarian, and next

15. Ibid., 85.
16. Ibid., 90.

to Augustus's lowered hand is an eagle.[17] In another panel emperor Claudius (reigned 41–54 CE) strides across land and sea, suggesting, with no subtlety, that "the exalted emperor has brought prosperity to the world—fertility to the land and safety to the sea."[18] There were similar complexes throughout Asia Minor. Ephesus itself had an extensive building project on behalf of the emperors.

Image of Emperor Claudius striding across earth and sea from Aphrodisias. Used by permission, Roger B. Ulrich.

3. THE EMPEROR CULT
AND JOHN'S ECOLOGICAL PERSPECTIVE

How should we coordinate these details of the emperor cult with an environmental reading of John's apocalypse? John engages in a battle of imaginations for who controls the universe. This is reminiscent of the same challenge the authors of *1 Enoch* faced in the context of Hellenistic propaganda. Indeed, the propaganda employed by Rome finds its roots in the Hellenistic period. We see the contours of this battle in

17. See R. R. R. Smith, "The Imperial Reliefs from the Sebasteion at Aphrodisias," *The Journal of Roman Studies* 77 (1987): plate IV.

18. Friesen, *Imperial Cults*, 92.

Revelation 7:9-17. A great multitude, so large it could not be counted, assembles around the throne. They cry out in a loud voice: "Salvation belongs to our God who is seated on the throne, and to the Lamb!" (7:10). The text goes on to describe the safety, security, guidance, and sustenance that will come from God and the lamb (9:15-17). Such claims directly challenge the propaganda of Rome's emperor cult. John's God is the true god, his proclamation thick with political overtones. John offers a clash of kingdoms. Those whom Rome has destroyed will not be abandoned (7:13-14) and Rome only appears to be in control. John's vision of God's power reveals who really runs the universe: "I saw one like the Son of Man, clothed with a long robe and with a golden sash across his chest . . . he placed his right hand on me, saying, 'Do not be afraid; I am the first and the last, and the living one. I was dead, and see, I am alive forever and ever; and I have the keys of Death and of Hades'" (Rev 1:13-14; 17-18).

The claims of the Roman emperors and those who established cults in their honor were cosmic in scope—they ruled earth, land, and sea. Their rule was accompanied by heavenly portents such as comets.[19] We should not be surprised, then, to see the way in which the entire natural environment is similarly caught up in the drama of John's Revelation. The words of Revelation 6 become quite striking in light of the propaganda seen in the statuary from Aphrodisias:

> When he opened the sixth seal, I looked, and there came a great earthquake; the sun became black as sackcloth, the full moon became like blood, and the stars of the sky fell to the earth as the fig tree drops its winter fruit when shaken by a gale. The sky vanished like a scroll rolling itself up, and every mountain and island was removed from its place. (Rev 6:12-14)

This language uses the same symbols as Rome's propaganda: moon, stars, and unexplainable portents like earthquakes. The elements of the cosmos are employed to represent sovereignty. In John's mind, those elements that Rome claimed to rule are obliterated and transformed.

---

19. For example, Julius Caesar was associated with a spectacular comet in 44 BCE. See Lewis A. Licht and John T. Ramsey, *The Comet of 44 B.C. and Caesar's Funeral Games* (Atlanta: Scholars Press, 1997).

This backdrop of Roman imperial propaganda can help us begin to make sense of John's treatment of cosmic imagery, which otherwise might lead to skepticism about Revelation's role in an environmental ethic. God sets loose destructive forces on the whole cosmos. In its ancient context, this becomes more understandable. The things being said about the emperor, according to John, were an affront to the true God's control of the universe. Rather than setting the resolution of this conflict in current time and space, John envisions something more drastic. The whole of creation will fold up on itself and God will create something new.

II. The Environmental Situation of the Roman Empire

The problematic environmental situation we discussed in the Hellenistic period in chapter two only continues to worsen during the Roman period. Deforestation, water and air pollution, habitat destruction, and waste management all continue to be serious problems.[20] In this next section, we will explore two specific instances in which the Roman Empire was wreaking environmental havoc on the earth and how John may have been responding to such destruction.

1. MINING IN THE ROMAN CONTEXT

Much of Rome's destruction of the environment was driven by its economic system. The earth often bore the brunt of Rome's desires. To take one example, mining was essential to Rome's economics and was practiced on a scale the world had not seen before.[21] Pliny the Elder (d. 79 CE) describes an exhausted mine that was deliberately caved in:

20. Each of these areas is given extensive discussion in Donald J. Hughes, *Environmental Problems of the Greeks and Romans: Ecology in the Ancient Mediterranean* (Baltimore: Johns Hopkins University Press, 2014).

21. For example, Pliny offers a description of how to smelt many different types and colors of bronze, and the best conditions under which to do so (Pliny the Elder, *Natural History*, vol. 9, trans. H. Rackham, Loeb Classical Library [Cambridge, MA: Harvard University Press, 1952], 34.20).

When the work is completely finished, beginning with the last, they cut through, at the tops, the supports of the arched roofs. A crack gives warning of a crash, and the only person who notices it is the sentinel on a pinnacle of the mountain . . . The fractured mountain falls asunder in a wide gap, with a crash which it is impossible for human imagination to conceive, and likewise with an incredibly violent blast of air. The miners gaze as conquerors upon the collapse of Nature (*spectant victores ruinam naturae*).[22]

The scars from such activity are still visible in some places today.[23]

Mining operations often impacted water sources. For example, Pliny also describes the diversion and channeling of water to places where the miners needed it for their work (*Nat.* 33.21.74-78). Noxious elements such as lead, mercury, and arsenic polluted waterways after hydraulic mining or through runoff and drainage.[24] Mining also polluted the air. Lucretius, a poet and philosopher (d. 55 BCE), describes the problem of air pollution for miners:

What stenches [the mine] breathes out underground! And what poison gold mines may exhale! How strange they make men's faces, how they change their color! Have you not seen or heard how they are wont to die in a short time and how the powers of life fail those whom the strong force of necessity imprisons in such work? All these effluences, then, earth sends steaming forth, and breathes them out into the open and the clear spaces of heaven. (*De Rerum Natura* 6.810-15)[25]

Archeological evidence supports Lucretius's observations that working conditions were abhorrent. Excavations have discovered people buried alive in collapses.[26] Pliny says that the miners do not see the daylight for many months (*Nat.* 33.21.70). He also discusses sudden collapses, claiming that it would be safer to try to get pearls from the depths of the sea because "so much more dangerous have we made the earth" (*Nat.* 33.21.70).

22. Pliny, *Natural History*, vol. 9, 33.21.72–73
23. Hughes, *Environmental Problems*, 144.
24. Ibid., 145.
25. Here I follow the translation in ibid., 145.
26. Ibid., 145.

Mining and the smelting of metals required enormous amounts of wood, which exacerbated deforestation. At the same time, ancient technology limited the depth a mine could reach, and so they were often quickly exhausted. This sent the empire looking farther and farther afield for new minerals and metals and the forests needed to process them. The thirst for the goods of the earth (trees and precious metals) pushed the Romans to expand their territory, perhaps beyond what they could sustain. Even with new resources, there were sometimes shortages. Pliny reports that in Campania (central Italy) bronze was being made with coal instead of charcoal, because of "their shortage of wood" (*Nat.* 34.96.97). The mining operations of the empire are just one small aspect of their economic program, but they clearly had environmental impacts and drove Rome farther afield for the materials themselves and for the fuel to process them.

In Revelation 9, the earth bears the brunt of apocalyptic scenarios. A star falls to earth, opening a pit that smokes like a furnace: "he [i.e., the angel] opened the shaft of the bottomless pit, and from the shaft rose smoke like the smoke of a great furnace, and the sun and the air were darkened with the smoke from the shaft. Then from the smoke came locusts on the earth" (Rev 9:2-3).

John has a variety of influences that help him produce a text such as this. The preceding woe (8:13) finds a deep biblical tradition in the Old Testament (for example, Isa 3:9-11) and is a form of speech used by Jesus (such as in Luke 6:24-26). Locusts provide an obvious link with the story of Moses and Pharaoh in the book of Exodus (Exod 10:1-20). Given the role of the earth in Roman propaganda and the devastation of the earth in the mining industry, however, it seems plausible that John is influenced also by environmental factors. John's smoking pit in 9:1-6 is reminiscent of Lucretius's description of the mines that belch smoke. Smoking underground chambers and polluted waters were part of his experience of Roman rule, direct by-products of the mining industry.[27] John, like Pliny the Elder, notices

---

27. Scholars have long noticed parallels between the details of John's Apocalypse and his Roman context. See Paul Barnett, "Polemical Parallelism: Some Further Reflections on the Apocalypse," *JSNT* 35 (1989): 111–20; and Christopher Frilingos, *Spectacles of Empire: Monsters, Martyrs, and the Book of Revelation* (Philadelphia: University of Pennsylvania Press, 2004).

the devastation wrought on the land.[28] John does not necessarily turn to the natural world because he wants to depict its destruction, but because its destruction was already part of his upbringing.

2. ANIMAL SPECTACLES
AND THEIR ENVIRONMENTAL PROBLEMS

Rome is famous for its gladiators, thanks in part to Hollywood. Movies such as *Spartacus* and *Gladiator* lionize heroes in our minds. Gladiators performed in violent shows meant to entertain the populace, to flaunt individual wealth, and to give honor to the emperor. The crowd sat in clearly demarcated social stratification. Rome's spectacles were tightly organized yet unpredictable. They were a microcosm of Rome itself.

The Roman games took several forms. The *munera* (a word that refers to something done on behalf of the public good) were the traditional gladiatorial games. These usually involved humans pitted against each other in various types of structured combat. Sometimes arenas were filled with water and great naval battles were acted out. Martial hints that they were gripping and convincing, telling someone unfamiliar with such games that they will think they had gazed upon the true ocean.[29] Another common part of the games was called *venationes*, which means something like "wild animal hunts." All manner of beasts were used in these games, the larger and more exotic the better: lions, tigers, elephants, leopards, hippos, and bears. Animals were usually pitted against other animals, but in some cases human gladiators were involved.

28. It is impossible to prove that John would have had direct experience of Roman mines or quarries. Mines and quarries outside of Roman Spain and Britain are "not well documented." See Alfred Michael Hirt, *Imperial Mines and Quarries in the Roman World: Organizational Aspects 27 BC–AD 235* (Oxford: Oxford University Press, 2010), 32. We have evidence of mines and quarries in Phrygia in west-central Anatolia. The marble from Phrygia would most likely have made its way to the harbor in Ephesos (ibid., 116).

29. See Martial, *Epigrams, Spectacles*, trans. D. R. Shackleton Bailey, Loeb Classical Library (Cambridge, MA: Harvard University Press, 1993), 24, where he says that the unfamiliar person will respond to an amphitheater's naval battle by saying, "here but now was sea."

Image of a gladiator and a leopard from a floor mosaic uncovered in Nennig, Germany. Although this image dates from after the book of Revelation (the late second to early third centuries), it depicts the kind of violence regularly experienced in Roman arenas. Image by Carole Raddato, used by permission.

a. Environmental impact of venationes

Venationes destroyed a mind-boggling number of animals. For example, at the festival opening the Coliseum in Rome (80 CE), there were one hundred days of spectacles. During this time 9,000 animals were killed. In 108 CE the emperor Trajan held contests that included 9,000 gladiators and over 11,000 animals were killed.[30]

The killing of so many animals devastated animal populations in the ancient world. A series of letters between Cicero and his friend Marcus Caelius Rufus demonstrates this. Cicero was governor in Cilicia, a remote province of what is today central Turkey. Rufus was in Rome and needed panthers in order to stage spectacular *venationes* there, so he wrote to Cicero to ask him for panthers. Rufus seems to think that the remote location of Cilicia would have them in abundance. Cicero responds that his best hunter came up empty because "there is a remarkable scarcity of panthers."[31] There is no reason to doubt Cicero's words here. In another letter, he laments the loss of

30. Jo-Ann Shelton, *As the Romans Did: A Source Book in Roman Social History* (New York: Oxford University Press, 1988), 344. Also Roland Auguet, *Cruelty and Civilization: The Roman Games* (London: Allen and Unwin, 1972), 107.

31. Shelton, *As the Romans Did*, 348.

human life in the spectacles and asks how it can be fun to watch a wild animal be stabbed repeatedly by a hunting spear. The particular games of which he was speaking saw the death of five hundred lions. The elephants came last, about which he says: "the mob of spectators was greatly impressed, but showed no real enjoyment. In fact, a certain sympathy arose for the elephants, and a feeling that there was a kind of affinity between that large animal and the human race."[32]

The demand for more beasts led to them being captured in more distant parts of the empire. Strabo records the effect this had on the Numidians in North Africa. He says that the native people there had always lived a nomadic existence. It is only with Roman domination and their systematic destruction of the region's wildlife that the Numidians could not sustain their traditional way of life. They transformed into farmers and citizens (Strabo, *Geogr.* 17.3.15). The whole empire was the hunting ground supplying the *venationes*. As Roland Auguet says in an attempt to summarize its scope: "It would have been possible richly to endow all the zoological gardens of Europe with the animals collected at Rome for a single great hunt."[33]

After learning about the *venationes,* you might wonder: what did they do with all those dead animals? While our ancient sources rarely give explicit answer to this question, it seems likely that some people would eat them. The early Christian writer Tertullian (d. 240 CE) suggests that carcasses from the *venationes* were eaten:

> [What of] those who dine on the flesh of wild animals from the arena, keen on the meat of boar or stag? That boar in his battle has wiped the blood off him whose blood he drew; that stag has wallowed in the blood of a gladiator. The bellies of the very bears are sought, full of raw and undigested human flesh.[34]

Another story comes from Apuleius's Latin novel *The Golden Ass.* He tells of a certain Demochares who went to great expense to put

32. Ibid., 347.

33. Auguet, *Cruelty and Civilization*, 107.

34. Tertullian, *Apology*, trans. T. R. Glover and Gerald H. Rendall, Loeb Classical Library No. 250 (Cambridge, MA: Harvard University Press, 1931), 9.11. Tertullian may be less than a reliable source on this point. He intends to attack the Greco-Roman culture that surrounds him. He also lived about one hundred years later than John. He seems most concerned here about the cannibalism that could result when people eat the meat left over from the *venationes*.

on a gladiator show. He had spent his last penny acquiring a large number of bears for the show. Apuleius explains how this did not work out very well:

> The bears, wearied by their long captivity, emaciated by the summer heat, and enervated by idle inactivity, succumbed to a sudden epidemic, so that scarcely one remained. You could see the hulks of half-dead beasts cast up like wrecks in street after street. Thereupon the common herd [i.e., people], compelled by sordid poverty and monotony of diet to seek any disgusting addition of free food for their shrunken bellies, fell on this feast which lay everywhere.[35] (*Metam.* 4.14)

Consumption of such meat may seem uncivilized to us, like the stereotypes of people who eat road kill. Most ancient diets, however, were protein deficient. Only the rich, rulers, and elites had regular access to meat. While distribution of meat after a spectacle would not have solved this problem, a populace accustomed to eating only grains and legumes—those with what Apuleius called "monotony of diet"—would have met it with alacrity.

Meat distribution at a spectacle fits into a larger pattern of meat availability at religious festivals. In the ancient world, the meat from sacrifices was rarely burned in a whole holocaust. In most cases it was consumed on site as part of the celebration. Other times this meat was sold in the marketplace. Sometimes this sacrificial meat was distributed to the people free of charge. Religious meat was an important part of the social, religious, and economic fabric of the ancient world.

The distribution of free meat to the masses would have had significant persuasive value. It was a chance for the emperor or whoever convened the games or religious festival to practice benefaction to the crowds. Free distributions of meat would not have offset protein deficiency in practical terms, but "in symbolic terms, they meant that at times an unemployed plebeian could still put meat on the table."[36]

35. Apuleius, *The Golden Ass*, trans. P. G. Walsh (Oxford: Oxford University Press, 1994).

36. Donald G. Kyle, "Animal Spectacles in Ancient Rome: Meat and Meaning," in *Sport in the Greek and Roman Worlds*, vol. 2, *Greek Athletic Identities and Roman Sports and Spectacle*, ed. Thomas F. Scanlon (Oxford: Oxford University Press, 2014), 291.

b. Symbolic value of spectacles

The Roman author Plutarch tells a story about the general Pompey and his defeat of the Numidians in Africa. After defeating the enemy, Pompey wanted to make the natives and the animals feel a healthy fear and respect of the Romans, which had been waning:

> He marched through the country for many days, conquered all who came in his way, and made potent and terrible again the Barbarians' fear of the Romans, which had reached a low ebb. Nay, he declared that even the wild beasts in African lairs must not be left without experience of the courage and strength of the Romans, and therefore spent a few days in hunting lions and elephants.[37]

A story like this suggests that the "systematic destruction of animals" was "beneficial" to Rome.[38] In other words, Roman propaganda could be expressed through their treatment of animals.

The *venationes* were not just for entertainment. They held significant symbolic value for the Romans. They demonstrated concretely the power of the emperor and the wealth of those who supported such games. Killing a lion in the center of Rome was a huge expense and was considered by Rome to be "the symbol of their complete power over the universe."[39] Domination over wild animals also underscored social domination. In the *venationes* cruel and destructive animals were got rid of, and the "process showed both how man controlled nature and how Rome controlled the world."[40] Like the obelisks that Romans brought back from Egypt and erected in their capitol, the "rich variety of animals really illustrated the geographical expansion of Rome's influence."[41]

Venationes embodied myth and religion as well. Sometimes the animals were used to act out Greek myths, which would set the

---

37. Plutarch, *Pompey*, in *Plutarch's Lives* V, trans. Bernadotte Perrin, Loeb Classical Library (Cambridge, MA: Harvard University Press, 1917), 12.

38. Christos Potamianos, "The Function of the Roman Spectacle in Ephesos" (MA thesis, University of California, Santa Barbara, 2011), 17.

39. Auguet, *Cruelty and Civilization*, 111–12.

40. Ingvild Saelid Gilhus, *Animals, Gods, and Humans: Changing Attitudes to Animals in Greek, Roman, and Early Christian Thought* (London: Routledge, 2006), 34.

41. Ibid., 34.

spectacle into a "cosmic universal context."[42] We also have clear evidence, especially in Roman Asia, that games were put on by priests or officials of the emperor cult.[43]

The display of *venationes* became a microcosm of those very things Rome wanted to be true throughout their vast empire: "The arena was where Roman society dealt not just with the chaos represented by wild beasts and of crime, but also the chaos of death. It was a symbol of the ordered world, the cosmos; it was the place where the civilized world confronted lawless nature."[44]

c. John's experience of venationes and his response

Not everyone in the ancient world was happy about spectacles and what they represented. In Athens, some leaders rejected the changes made to the theater of Dionysus that made it viable for spectacles. The theater was seen as a sacred space. Apollonius of Tyana, an Athenian sage active toward the end of the first century, refused to enter the theater because the place was filled with gore (Philostratus, *Vita Apol.* 4.22). He was amazed that the goddess Athena had not fled the Acropolis because of all the blood being shed right under her nose.

Jews in the first century had similar reactions. The Jewish historian Josephus (37–100 CE) tells a story in which the gladiatorial and animal games enticed, but also challenged, Jewish populations in the first century. Herod Agrippa (d. 44 CE), the grandson of Herod the Great, built a theater in Jerusalem and held spectacles that went "farther in departing from the native customs" and "gradually corrupted the ancient way of life" (*Ant.* 15.8.1). The theater was filled with inscriptions and statues honoring Caesar, and Josephus takes the time to discuss animals specifically:

> There was also a supply of wild beasts, a great many lions and other animals having been brought together for him, such as were of extraordinary strength or of very rare kinds. When the

42. Thomas Wiedemann, *Emperors and Gladiators* (London: Routledge, 1992), 85.
43. Michael J. D. Carter, "The Presentation of Gladiatorial Spectacles in the Greek East: Roman Culture and Greek Identity" (PhD diss., McMaster University, 1999), 198–99.
44. Wiedemann, *Emperors and Gladiators*, 179.

practice began of involving them in combat with one another or setting condemned men to fight against them, foreigners were astonished at the expense and at the same time entertained by the dangerous spectacle, but to the natives it meant an open break with the customs held in honour by them. For it seemed glaring impiety to throw men to wild beasts for the pleasure of other men as spectators, and it seemed a further impiety to change their established ways for foreign practices.[45]

Some later Christians, such as Clement of Alexandria and Tertullian, offer critiques of Roman games similar to that of Josephus. We are within the bounds of reason to turn to John's apocalypse to see how experience of *venationes* may have contributed to the context that shaped his worldview.[46]

i. First Response: God is the creator and ruler of these animals

John leaves no doubt that God is the creator of the universe, the one who controls everything and who deserves worship for such power. Following many texts from the Old Testament, John routinely praises God for creating all things. In chapter 4, twenty-four elders around God's throne sing:

> You are worthy, our Lord and God,
>   to receive glory and honor and power,
> for you created all things,
>   and by your will they existed and were created. (4:11)

The elders lay down their crowns, symbols of earthly power, and yield the stage to four living creatures. These creatures, like a lion, ox, eagle, and human, seem to be "representatives of the world of

---

45. Josephus, *Jewish Antiquities 2–13*, trans. H. St. J. Thackeray and Ralph Marcus, Loeb Classical Library (Cambridge, MA: Harvard University Press, 1943), 15.8.1. Josephus goes on to explain that the Jews were also concerned about the statues that were given out as prizes, which were against their laws.

46. There should be little doubt that John would have been aware of and experienced *venationes*. The theater in Ephesus was retrofitted to make such games possible (Potamianos, "Roman Spectacle in Ephesos," 30; Frilingos, *Spectacles of Empire*, 29). A relief sculpture from the theater depicts the god Eros in combat with a bear (Potamianos, "Roman Spectacle in Ephesos," 17).

earthly creatures."[47] The four living creatures that hover around the throne supplant the human figures. John's depiction here of the heavenly realm, where all is as it should be, is noticeably nonanthropocentric; the "human has no privilege or precedence here."[48] In a context where the Roman Empire was asserting its domination over all of creation, and in the *venationes* engaging in horrible exploitation of animals, the praise becomes a dramatic counter-ideology with deep political ramifications. Roman designs on domination of the animal kingdom are an affront to the role of God as creator and sustainer.

Revelation 5 begins with a vision of a scroll with seven seals in the right hand of the one seated on the throne (5:1). John weeps because no one is able to open the scroll, until he realizes that the lamb is worthy (5:6-8). This leads to a vision of many thousands of angels, along with the elders and four living creatures, who sing with full voice about how the lamb is worthy (5:12). Then the song to the lamb expands to include, "every creature in heaven and on earth and under the earth and in the sea, and all that is in them" (5:13). The language here evokes the creation story in Genesis 1. By specifically naming those creatures on the earth, under the earth, and in the sea, the author encapsulates all of creation, not just humans, as those who recognize the sovereignty of God on the throne and the lamb.

To a community familiar with the *venationes*, songs of praise such as those in Revelation 4–5 would take on a particular resonance. They challenge the Roman claims to sovereignty as represented in the *venationes* and the way it was manifested in territorial expansion and exploitation of the animal kingdom. As we saw in the Book of Watchers, John here offers an ecological critique of the Roman Empire by undermining the conceptual basis on which the propaganda of the *venationes* rests.[49]

47. Richard Bauckham, *Living with Other Creatures: Green Exegesis and Theology* (Waco, TX: Baylor University Press, 2011): 177.

48. Ibid., 183.

49. See a similar argument by Barbara R. Rossing, "River of Life in God's New Jerusalem: An Ecological Vision for the Earth's Future," *Mission Studies* 16 (1999): 136–56. She refers to an "astute ecological critique" of Rome in Revelation in the context of ancient deforestation.

ii. Second Response: Do not eat meat from the venationes

John also would likely have been aghast at the prospect of eating the meat left over from the *venationes*. Near the beginning of Revelation, John is instructed by an angel to write letters to seven churches.[50] These letters give us some of the most direct access to the socioeconomic situation of the communities to which John was writing. They faced a variety of challenges and are praised or chastised for their varying degrees of obedience and endurance. In the letter to Pergamum (2:12-17) and the letter to Thyatira (2:18-29), John discusses the issue of food that has been sacrificed to an idol (2:15, 20). Eating this food, for John, is akin to idolatry and fornication. It is like sleeping with a prostitute (2:14, 22).[51]

John's rejection of food sacrificed to an idol has long been understood as a rejection of the sacrificial system of polytheism and its gods. We have now seen, however, how important the *venationes* were for Roman religion and propaganda. John may have made no distinction between food available at a festival in honor of Artemis and that distributed freely after the *venationes* were finished. Because of the way politics, economics, and religion were enmeshed, his rejection of eating meat after the *venationes* would have been total. It seems possible that John rejected eating religious meat because he rejected Rome's claims to domination of the animals of God's creation. John rejects outright the exploitation and destruction of the animal kingdom, which finds its true ownership in God the creator.

iii. Third Response: The animals will devour YOU!

Revelation 6 narrates the breaking of the seven seals. With each of the first four, riders emerge on colored horses: white, red, black, and

---

50. Commands to write something down are common in apocalyptic and revelatory contexts (see Tob 12:20; *1 En.* 13:4). The letters at the beginning of Revelation also evoke the epistolary correspondence of the apostle Paul.

51. Readers of John's Apocalypse must always be aware of the danger of misogyny. When John wants to conjure the worst thing imaginable, he often turns to a seductive woman. There are many good treatments of this topic. See, for example, Tina Pippin, *Death and Desire: The Rhetoric of Gender in the Apocalypse of John* (Louisville, KY: Westminster John Knox, 1992); Amy-Jill Levine and Maria Mayo Robbins, eds., *A Feminist Companion to the Apocalypse of John* (London: T&T Clark, 2009); and Barbara R. Rossing, *The Choice Between Two Cities: Whore, Bride, and Empire in the Apocalypse* (Harrisburg, PA: Trinity Press International, 1999).

pale green. They are given dominion by God to destroy various aspects of the earth; they act "within God's direct sphere of influence."[52] The implements with which they destroy are drawn from the Roman Empire, which will help us understand further John's interaction with wild animals.

The white horse emerges with a rider carrying a bow and wearing a crown. His crown "was given" to him (6:2). The passive voice leaves the actor ambiguous (in other words, we do not know who gave him the crown). In the Hebrew Bible and in many New Testament texts, including as many as twenty-two instances in Revelation, such constructions assume God as the agent of action.[53] We call this grammatical construction a "divine passive." The bow represents the war implement of the Parthians, one of Rome's worst enemies.[54] It is also possible the bow is meant to evoke the god Apollo, since it was his attribute in ancient iconography. The bow and crown are images drawn from John's context with which most people would have been familiar, emphasizing power and might. John takes those images and turns them back on the powerful, as the horse and its rider conquer.

The red horse and its rider take away peace. Roman peace (*pax romana*) was foundational for Roman propaganda. Here (Rev 6:4) God's agent takes it away. The red horse and its rider "are given" a great sword. This evokes an official form of Roman capital punishment called the "right of the sword" (*ius gladii*), meted out exclusively by the emperor in Rome or provincial governors to whom the power was granted.[55] John rips a sword of judgment from the hands of Rome and wields it back on those from whom it was taken. There is no more *pax romana*.

The fourth horse (pale green) and its rider are followed by Death and Hades. They are given (another divine passive) authority to kill one fourth of the earth with sword, famine, and pestilence, and "by the wild animals" (6:8). John's words here may be influenced by traditions in the

---

52. Brian K. Blount, *Revelation: A Commentary* (Louisville, KY: Westminster John Knox Press, 2009), 124.

53. David E. Aune, *Revelation: 1–5*, WBC 52A (Grand Rapids, MI: Zondervan, 1997), 394.

54. Blount, *Revelation*, 125.

55. Aune, *Revelation: 1–5*, 396.

Hebrew Bible. The words sword, famine, and pestilence are a common "triad of afflictions."[56] Occasionally, wild animals are included among these afflictions. We also find references to wild animals as judgment in the Hebrew Bible, in other Jewish literature, and in some ancient near eastern curses.[57] Scholars have not looked to John's Roman context to help explain the wild beasts in Revelation 6:8. Since most of the implements of destruction are stolen from Rome's own dominance and propaganda, such a background seems quite likely. Within the context of Revelation 6, it makes sense to have God co-opt and turn against Rome the very thing that was originally its means of destroying others. John takes the emblem of control Rome perpetuated and the violence it perpetrated and sets it loose on the earth.

III. The Sea, the Sea

John's Apocalypse is dominated by the sea. The book opens with John on the island of Patmos, surrounded by the sea. It ends oppositely: a new heaven and new earth in which "the sea was no more" (21:1). Revelation uses the Greek word for "sea" (θάλασσα) twenty-six times, almost twice as many as the next closest book in the New Testament. A cursory reading of the Apocalypse could lead to the conclusion that John hated the sea. God repeatedly pelts the sea with the same cataclysms experienced by other elements of creation. Is John's depiction of the sea irrevocably negative? How can we read a book that eliminates the sea and have it contribute positively to ecological consciousness? As we will see, John's interpretations of the sea are dependent upon the context in which he lived.[58] John's depiction of the sea derives from Rome's claims to dominate it, and, at the same time, from Jewish creation mythology. From these aspects of his upbringing, John employs the sea as one of his primary metaphors throughout the Apocalypse.

56. Ibid., 402.

57. Ibid., 403; and Blount, *Revelation*, 131.

58. Here I have been helped by Jonathan Moo, "The Sea That Is No More: Rev 21:1 and the Function of Sea Imagery in the Apocalypse of John," *Novum Testamentum* 51, no. 2 (2009): 148–67.

1. THE SEA AS THE ORIGIN OF CHAOS

Most of this chapter has explored the Roman Empire as the constitutive component of John's upbringing, something he perceived as negative and against which he reacts. The traditions of ancient Judaism were just as formative. John draws upon Jewish creation mythology to depict the sea as the origin of chaos and opposition to God.

The oldest creation story in the ancient near east—one that the Jewish people shared with their neighbors—describes a god who creates by destroying a mythological sea monster.[59] This myth is much older than the ordered creation in Genesis 1. Psalm 74, for instance, understands creation as a primordial battle:

> Yet God my King is from of old,
>> working salvation in the earth.
> You divided the sea by your might;
>> you broke the heads of the dragons in the waters.
> You crushed the heads of Leviathan;
>> you gave him as food for the creatures of the wilderness. (Ps 74:12-14)

In this myth, God calms the chaotic waters and destroys the many-headed beast that roils them. This creates the peace and space necessary for life to exist. Similar vestiges of the myth can be seen in Isaiah 51, Job 41, and other places as well.

One of the ways apocalyptic literature expresses its understanding of evil is by suggesting that these monsters and the chaotic sea from which they come have reasserted themselves. In the book of Daniel, an apocalyptic text, beasts rise from the sea: "I, Daniel, saw in my vision by night the four winds of heaven stirring up the great sea, and four great beasts came up out of the sea. . ." (Dan 7:2). The author suggests that the experience of evil is like the reemergence of a primordial foe that causes chaos and destruction.

---

59. For example, the Babylonian myth called *Enuma Elish*. See Richard J. Clifford, "The Roots of Apocalypticism in Near Eastern Myth," in *The Encyclopedia of Apocalypticism*, vol. 1, *The Origins of Apocalypticism in Judaism and Christianity*, ed. John J. Collins (New York: Continuum, 1998), 3–38.

John of Patmos knows this mythological tradition and intentionally employs it throughout the Apocalypse.[60] In chapter 13, a beast rises from the sea, a scene clearly influenced by Daniel chapter 7. This beast comes from the abyss (Greek ἄβυσσος), according to 11:7, an idea later recapitulated in 17:8. The sea for John is not just the Mediterranean that he saw from the Island of Patmos. This sea is the "primeval sea to which all other seas are linked."[61] Through these motifs, John refers to the old myth of combat between God and a primordial foe.

2. THE SEA AS ROME'S TERRITORY

John also uses the sea as a reference to the economic and militaristic power of the Roman Empire. In chapter 17 John sees a vision of a whore who rides on the beast. She is "seated on many waters" (17:1). References later in the chapter make clear that this woman represents Rome and her placement on the water indicates one source of Rome's power and wealth, which was its dominance of the sea. Chapter 18 reinforces this idea, expressed as a lament by those rich and powerful individuals who will be impoverished by Rome's downfall at the hand of God. Here it is worth quoting at length to understand the lament:

> And the merchants of the earth weep and mourn for her, since no one buys their cargo any more, cargo of gold, silver, jewels and pearls, fine linen, purple, silk and scarlet, all kinds of scented wood, all articles of ivory, all articles of costly wood, bronze, iron, and marble, cinnamon, spice, incense, myrrh, frankincense, wine, olive oil, choice flour and wheat, cattle and sheep, horses and chariots, slaves—and human lives.
> "The fruit for which your soul longed
>   has gone from you,
> and all your dainties and your splendor
>   are lost to you,
> never to be found again!"

---

60. Adela Yarbro Collins, *The Combat Myth in the Book of Revelation* (Missoula, MT: Scholars Press, 1976). Collins is careful to document the ways in which John may have had this myth mediated to him through traditions that are outside of the Old Testament texts. See also Moo, "The Sea That Is No More," 158.

61. Moo, "The Sea That Is No More," 156.

The merchants of these wares, who gained wealth from her, will stand far off, in fear of her torment, weeping and mourning aloud,

> "Alas, alas, the great city,
>> clothed in fine linen,
>>> in purple and scarlet
>> adorned with gold,
>>> with jewels, and with pearls!
> For in one hour all this wealth has been laid waste!"

And all shipmasters and seafarers, sailors and all whose trade is on the sea, stood far off and cried out as they saw the smoke of her burning,

> "What city was like the great city?"

And they threw dust on their heads, as they wept and mourned, crying out,

> "Alas, alas, the great city,
>> where all who had ships at sea
>> grew rich by her wealth!
> For in one hour she has been laid waste." (18:11-19)

These verses demonstrate the extent to which the sea was Rome's domain and its connection with economic power and control.[62] The specific items enumerated were among the greatest luxuries mentioned by ancient Roman writers who discussed extravagant wealth.[63] The list of goods demonstrates Rome's "addiction to consumption" that came at the "expense of the peoples of the empire."[64] When the landlocked new heavens and new earth arrive in chapters 21–22, we see a "pointed economic contrast" with Rome.[65] Removing the sea removes an essential element of the mechanism of Rome's exploitative, consumerist economy.

3. JOHN'S USE OF THE SEA EXPLAINED

These explorations help us understand John's view of the sea. It dominates his landscape, probably literally and certainly figuratively.

62. Barbara R. Rossing, "River of Life," 138–39.
63. Richard Bauckham, *Climax of Prophecy: Studies on the Book of Revelation* (Edinburgh: T&T Clark, 2000), 350–71.
64. Ibid., 368–69.
65. Rossing, "River of Life," 143.

While we rightly demur when we see how God in the Apocalypse destroys the sea and removes it altogether from the new creation, in John's context it might make some sense. His upbringing has led him to view it in a certain way. John's view of the sea is refracted through the double lens of ancient creation mythology and Roman economic exploitation. There is no indication that the sea itself is adversarial to God or God's people.[66] The problem for John is that the extent of Rome's exploits made the sea no longer God's domain. Rome, as the beast who is given authority from the devil, rises from the sea. It is Rome's domain. Once we realize this, then some of the features of his depiction of the sea become more understandable.

The glass-like sea in 4:6 provides a symbol quite the opposite of the chaotic primordial waters: "and in front of the throne there is something like a sea of glass, like crystal." In a context that contains a rainbow and extensive worship of God, one finds a promise embedded in this vision. Creatures and elders praise God for God's power. What better image to communicate that praiseworthy power than a sea without a ripple? As Jonathan Moo says, the image of the glassy sea "may well hint at the Lord's sovereignty over its stilled waters."[67] In heaven (where this vision takes place) all is well; there is no chaos. While this image of the sea may be unrealistic and unnatural, it has deep symbolic importance—the power of God, represented symbolically in the glassy sea, promises a good future. The beast does not threaten heaven, a situation that God will implement on earth imminently.[68]

John's expulsion of the sea from the new heaven and the new earth likely draws from traditions about the escape from Pharaoh in the Old Testament. In chapter 15, John sees another glassy sea (this one mixed with fire). Those who observed the destruction of

---

66. *1 Enoch* 101 provides an interesting contrast to Revelation on this point. The author of this text suggests that sinners ought to fear the sea like sailors do. Sinners ought to fear God like sailors fear the sea.

67. Moo, "The Sea That Is No More," 153.

68. Craig R. Koester suggests that John does not interact with the chaotic sea myth in removing the sea from the new creation. He points out that both the sea and the earth are places from which evil springs in Revelation (see 13:1, 11). John does not single out the sea because "both sea and land are susceptible to evil in Revelation." *Revelation: A New Translation with Introduction and Commentary*, ed. John J. Collins, Anchor Bible Series (New Haven, CT: Yale University Press, 2014), 796.

the beast stand on the edge of this sea and sing a song of Moses and of the lamb. They laud God for power, justice, and might (15:3-4). These words recall the song of Moses and the Israelites in Exodus 15, in which they praise God for how God delivered them from Pharaoh as they passed through the Red Sea. John reinforces the exodus imagery through the bowls of wrath in the next chapter (chap. 16) that evoke the plagues God sends on Pharaoh: water to blood, darkness, skin sores, and abundant amphibians.[69] When seen with this backdrop, John's treatment of the sea takes on a whole new set of resonances. In the exodus story Israel's deliverance took place in the sea. Its removal symbolizes the obliteration of a barrier between the people and that which God has promised them. As Jonathan Moo says, the absence of the sea from the new creation "could imply the accomplishment of a second exodus for the exiled people of God."[70] If the sea is no more, then every step finds dry ground, safety, and a path toward the promised land.

We are right to be concerned about Revelation's words about the sea. An interpreter, at the same time, ought to take the time to understand them. John's environmental personality, at first blush, seems problematic. He presents the sea as the origin of evil and removes it from the new creation. We now see the complexity of his argument, which draws upon components of his context in the Roman Empire, his knowledge of the texts and traditions of Judaism, all combined with his belief in a God who has true power and rules the universe. According to John, if the sea were to exist at all, then there would always remain the threat that chaos could return and threaten God and God's people again; it would always remain possible that "evil might spring up in an otherwise good creation."[71] For John, the

69. The plagues that follow the bowls of wrath in Revelation 16 do not map perfectly onto the story of Moses, Aaron, and Pharaoh in Exodus. John wants to evoke them, not copy them slavishly. John's use could also have been mediated by another textual tradition. The story and themes of the Exodus were represented in a variety of ways. Psalm 78, for example, seems to list seven plagues, not ten (Ps 78:43-50).

70. Moo, "The Sea That Is No More," 155. Later in his article, Moo reinforces this argument by drawing upon resonances with Isaiah 43 and 51 as well (pp. 162–65).

71. Ibid., 166.

sea's removal emphasizes that the new creation is different from the first—the sea, the beast, and the power that it enlivens "will no longer pose any threat in the renewed cosmos . . . for all judgment will be past and salvation finally and definitively accomplished."[72]

In chapter 12 John suggests that what is happening is not the sea's fault at all:

> Rejoice then, you heavens
>   and those who dwell in them!
> But woe to the earth and the sea,
>   for the devil has come down to you
> with great wrath,
>   because he knows that his time is short! (Rev 12:12)

The devil imposes wrath on the earth and sea. They suffer because of the devil's death throes. The sea does not deserve its suffering but endures it as an unfortunate consequence of the satanic forces that have infiltrated the world. To be sure, God and God's angels mete out most of the destruction, but only as a punishment and judgment that results because of the presence of evil. The destruction resembles the plagues of Egypt, which were meant to goad people to turn from their evil ways. Revelation also intends its cataclysms to lead to a change of ways, wishing that people would learn from them and "repent of the work of their hands" (9:20).

IV. Conclusion

When we step back and look at John's upbringing, the context in which he was forged, we see Roman propaganda claiming control of the universe and a variety of ways that that control was detrimental to the earth. In response to this, John does not offer a small fix. He offers instead a clash of kingdoms:

> The kingdom of the world has become the kingdom of our Lord
> and of his Messiah, and he will reign forever and ever. (11:15)

These strains, known to us from the Hallelujah Chorus in Handel's *Messiah*, establish the breadth of the critique and challenge John

---

72. Ibid., 167.

presents to the Roman Empire. In 11:18, the same voices note that the "nations raged" but that the time has come for God's wrath and for judgment. In addition, it is also time "for destroying those who destroy the earth" (Rev 11:18). Here John may be hinting at the environmental component of his critique of Rome. His purview extends beyond what Rome has done to humans, to include the whole earth and animals as well.

Once we recognize this environmental component of John's critique, other details in Revelation can be reinterpreted. Revelation 12:12 proclaims: "woe to the earth and the sea, for the devil has come down to you with great wrath." The word "woe" here is potentially very problematic from an ecological point of view. It suggests that God is complicit in wanting to destroy the earth. Barbara Rossing makes a convincing argument that the Greek word (οὐαί), translated in most Bibles as "woe," should really be understood as a lament.[73] The verse reads very differently if the voice from heaven proclaims: "*Alas* to the earth and sea." This translation suggests that John's intent was never to proclaim woe on the earth, but to lament over the fact that it is captive to Rome. In Rossing's words: "the book of Revelation laments Rome's exploitation of the entire world, its enslavement of both humans and nature by violent military conquest."[74] David Hawkin has built upon Rossing's work, concluding that John "shows a remarkable grasp of the link between economic injustice and ecological exploitation. But more than that, he also shows an understanding of the damage that Rome's hegemony has done to the environment."[75]

John's problems are still our problems today. We now live in the midst of the sixth great extinction in the history of our planet.[76] While John was not intending to predict our future, his insights into the exploitation of animals at the hands of empire anticipate a

73. Barbara R. Rossing, "Alas for the Earth! Lament and Resistance in Revelation 12," in *The Earth Story in the New Testament*, ed. Norman Habel and Vicky Balabanski (London: Sheffield Academic Press, 2002), 180–92.

74. Rossing, "Alas for the Earth," 191.

75. David J. Hawkin, "The Critique of Ideology in the Book of Revelation and its Implications for Ecology," *Ecotheology* 8 (2003): 169.

76. S. L. Pimm et al., "The Biodiversity of Species and Their Rates of Extinction, Distribution, and Protection," *Science* 344 (2014): 987.

consistent problem. John offers us what Stephen Moore calls "an apocalyptic uncovering of the already present future of our catastrophically theriocidal [i.e., wild animal killing] cultures."[77] In other words, we can draw a line from ancient destruction of animals to the sixth global extinction recognized today. Our infrastructure prevents migration. Our agriculture destroys habitat. The book of Revelation rejects the impact of human action on ecosystems and the ramifications for animals because such actions oppose the aims of God.

Moreover, we, like John, ought to lament over the sea's destruction. Overfishing, pollution, and even the noise from boats in the shipping industry all degrade the sea's ability to function.[78] Rising sea temperatures destroy coral and choke the ocean of oxygen.[79] The U.S. military's use of sonar causes disorientation in whale and dolphin pods, often leading to death on a large scale.[80] Consumerist economics and a mentality driven by empire create these problems. If we took John's words seriously in our world today, we ought to ask ourselves very hard questions every time we build an oil platform in the ocean, when we eat unsustainable fish, or when we buy an iPad

77. Stephen D. Moore, *Untold Tales from the Book of Revelation: Sex and Gender, Empire and Ecology* (Atlanta: Society of Biblical Literature Press, 2014), 242.

78. Vincent M. Janik and Paul M. Thompson, "Changes in Surfacing Patterns of Bottlenose Dolphins in Response to Boat Traffic," *Maritime Mammal Science* 12, no. 4 (1996): 597–602.

79. For data about climate change and coral, see O. Hoegh-Guldberg et al., "Coral Reefs Under Rapid Climate Change and Ocean Acidification," *Science* 318, no. 5857 (2007): 1737–1742. For oxygen levels and sea temperature, see Matthew C. Long, Curtis Deutsch, and Ito Taka, "Finding Forced Trends in Oceanic Oxygen: Trends in Dissolved Oxygen," *Global Biogeochemical Cycles* 30, no. 2 (2016): 381–97.

80. Lenny Berstein, "Panel Links Underwater Mapping Sonar to Whale Stranding for First Time," *Washington Post*, October 6, 2013, https://www .washingtonpost.com/national/health-science/panel-links-underwater -mapping-sonar-to-whale-stranding-for-first-time/2013/10/06/52510204 -2e8e-11e3-bbed-a8a60c601153_story.html. See also Ben Guarino, "Navy's Submarine Hunts are too Disturbing for Marine Life, California Court Rules," *Washington Post*, July 20, 2016, https://www.washingtonpost.com/news /morning-mix/wp/2016/07/20/navys-submarine-hunts-are-too-disturbing -for-marine-wildlife-california-federal-appeals-court-rules.

that has been shipped across the Pacific. The state of the sea today gives us plenty over which we can lament.

We do not need John's Apocalypse to tell us this—our modern ecological sciences can. What John provides is a profile of the deeper reasons and solutions. The problem is not with economics per se. The problem is with allegiances. John tells us that insatiable consumption and lust for wealth, at the expense of anything that stands in their way, is satanic, of the devil. Empire puts economic gain and domination ahead of Jesus's lordship. The problem is worship. Worship of the beast, its empire, and its economic program are the true cause of the problem:

> Also it [i.e., the second beast] causes all, both small and great, both rich and poor, both free and slave, to be marked on the right hand or the forehead, so that no one can buy or sell who does not have the mark. (Rev 13:16-17)

Proper worship of God will attune our ears to the problem and help us recognize that how we treat the sea has religious implications, and if we get that wrong, we run the risk of abandoning our allegiance to God. This means that the opposite is true—that if we claim to worship the true God, the one who created and controls the cosmos, then certain moral actions follow from that claim. There are ways of living that properly align with that worship. A way of living that sees the sea as a source of income, something to be exploited—whether wittingly or not—is not attuned to God. An approach to the natural environment that places affluence and accumulation of dainties above creatures and creation does not cohere with proper worship of God.

The essential problem, according to John, is one of allegiance and power. In God's kingdom, weakness and vulnerability rule, seen in the image of the slaughtered lamb (e.g., 5:6; 7:9). This mode of rule in the kingdom subverts the domination, exploitation, and violence meted out by Rome on its natural environment. Once we understand John's upbringing and how he depicted the destruction of the world because of his context, it becomes clear that the ecological "take away" is not to ape that destruction. The path offered by the lamb is one of defiant refusal to capitulate with the empire.

The apocalyptic ecology profiled by John will seem crazy in our modern context. As Steven Friesen says, "Revelation challenges any epistemology that signifies only in the mode of western rationality."[81] This means that John's perspective will clash with a modern empire, just as it did with the ancient one. John's prescription is not a list of small things everyone can do. John would scoff at our claims to save the earth by recycling, composting, driving a Prius, and taking shorter showers. John envisions a complete break from the ways that empire tramples creation in the name of economic progress and dominance. It is too late to change course; something wholly new must be mustered.

The Roman author Tacitus, writing at the end of the first century, said of Roman activities in Britannia: "they make a desert and call it peace."[82] John of Patmos would agree. Part of John's upbringing was the ecological devastation wrought by the Roman Empire and its fusion with religious propaganda and claims to global dominance. John's response is far from charitable. He gives Rome no benefit of the doubt. For his community, there is no gray area: you are either on the creator God's side or on the side of the destroyers.

This reminds me of playing board games with my kids. Once it becomes apparent that he will not win, my younger son does not cheat or connive a way to win. Instead, with a violent thrash, he overturns the board, tossing the pieces across the room. The game cannot be played anymore. John does not change the rules. Instead, the entire universe in which the game is being played will be undone. In John's vision of the new future that God will create, even the sea—the very basis of Rome's economic power—will be no more (Rev 21:1). With no sky, no sea, and a darkened moon and sun, those environmental and cosmological symbols of the emperors' reign disappear.[83] John overturns the board and scatters the playing pieces, rendering them useless.

81. Friesen, *Imperial Cults*, 216.

82. *Atque ubi solitudinem faciunt, pacem appellant.* Tacitus, *Dialogus, Agricola, Germania*, trans. W. Peterson and M. Hutton, Loeb Classical Library (Cambridge, MA: Harvard University Press, 1914), 30.

83. See Paul Barnett, "Polemical Parallelism," 111–20, who notes how Nero presented himself as Apollo Helios (Apollo of the Sun).

CHAPTER FOUR

Revelation's Career

Environmental Entanglement in Illuminated Manuscripts

> "Big mountain, wide river
> there's an ancient pull
> these tree trunks, these stream beds
> leave our bellies full"
> —The Decemberists

Visitors to Athens scrabble their way up the Acropolis to see one of the world's most famous structures: the Parthenon. A temple built to honor Athena in the fifth century BCE, the Parthenon still moves people to tears and sparks intellectual and artistic imaginations. But what is the Parthenon, really? The Parthenon has not played its original role—temple to Athena—since the fifth century CE. It was used as a Christian church dedicated to the Virgin Mary for one thousand years, as long as its dedication to Athena. It housed a mosque. It stored ammunition for the Turks. In the nineteenth century it was so neglected that Lord Elgin could chisel sculpture from its façade without raising much ire. Today it is little more than a museum—dilapidated marble that archeologists piece back together. There are many Parthenons.[1] The building has had a varied, complex, ever-changing career.

---

1. See Mary Beard's book: *The Parthenon* (Cambridge, MA: Harvard University Press, 2003), which discusses the various functions of the Parthenon across the centuries.

Biblical texts also have careers, a fact that biblical scholars are only beginning to recognize. Most scholarly study of the Bible has sought origins, the pristine moment in which a text was written and its author's meaning was conveyed. We like to "anchor" biblical texts in their original contexts so the author's meaning can be discerned. One might ask, however: who pulled up the anchor in the first place? How did they leave our harbor? Despite the best effort of scholars, biblical texts are "always found drifting through history, seemingly unanchored, usually witnessing to something" other than their original context.[2] This is as true for Revelation as for any book of the Bible. History reveals an Apocalypse whose rope has been cut, untethered from anything "John" intended. Biblical texts are not objects but objectiles.[3] They must be studied as "something for which movement and variation is a necessary quality."[4]

Seeking how Revelation is an objectile across time could lead one in a thousand directions. We could look at sculpture, painting, music, movies, political propaganda, Dungeons and Dragons, or theological treatises. The woodcuts of Albrecht Dürer (d. 1528) and Lucas Cranach (d. 1553), for example, interpret Revelation in the specific religious and political situation of their age, using the images to show their sympathy for the reforms of Martin Luther. In so doing, they set the images from Revelation in their own environmental context of fifteenth- and sixteenth-century Europe. William Blake, poet and artist, used the book of Revelation as a template for his critique of the industrial revolution in his poem "Jerusalem." He harkens back to an earlier time when England was verdant and contrasts it with the "dark satanic mills" that he sees destroying the landscape. The poem, inspired by Revelation, sees a time when Jesus will return to England and establish a Jerusalem that will be a "green and pleasant land."[5] Slightly less poetically, many of my students can

2. Brennan W. Breed, *Nomadic Text: A Theory of Biblical Reception History* (Bloomington: Indiana University Press, 2014), 76.

3. Ibid., 119. Here Breed says that biblical scholars ought to understand the Bible as an "objectile-text that moves and changes but that has local determinations, or particular texts and readings."

4. Ibid., 116–17.

5. For a good summary of the dizzying array of ways Revelation has been represented in art across the centuries, see Natasha O'Hear and Anthony O'Hear,

quote Revelation 21:6 because it appears at the beginning of the video game *Fallout 4.*

Given the multiplicity of options, I have chosen here to focus narrowly on one specific type of interpretation of Revelation: illuminated manuscripts. These are versions of the text of the book of Revelation, written by hand and accompanied by images that supplement the text. Some also contain written commentary on Revelation. I have chosen to focus on these illuminated manuscripts for two main reasons. First, we have examples of them from a variety of historical contexts and geographical locations. This chronological and geographic variety allows us to gain perspective on Revelation's varied career. Second, in most cases the art in these manuscripts includes florid artistic representations of the natural world. This beautiful art provides the opportunity to explore the relationship between Revelation and people's environmental imaginations in various times and places.

In this chapter we will explore four illuminated manuscripts, three from the medieval period and one that is modern. Those I have chosen seem very interested in depicting the natural world. Using a method called "visual exegesis," by which we will interpret the details of the art rather than the words of the text, we will ask eco-critical questions of these manuscripts. What impact did Revelation have on the ecological imagination of communities in various places? From the details we will find that rather than spawn destruction, Revelation evokes contemplation of the natural environment and sketches the way in which humans, God, and environment are all entangled together.

I. Medieval Illuminated Manuscripts of Revelation

Our modern age, five hundred years after the invention of the printing press, makes it hard to understand manuscripts in the medieval period. We scan and email PDFs. We expect our snapchats to be deleted immediately but want our tweets to reach the world instantly.

Picturing the Apocalypse: The Book of Revelation in the Arts over Two Millennia (Oxford: Oxford University Press, 2015).

Ancient writing was very different. The word "manuscript" literally means "handwritten." They were precious because of the time, effort, and resources needed to produce them. Most manuscripts were written for ecclesiastical use. Because of this, they were predominantly biblical and liturgical, often reproductions of the whole Bible or liturgically important sections of it, especially the Psalms and the gospels. In certain times and places, Revelation also received individual treatment. These clusters of manuscripts give us a wealth of imagery from which to explore Revelation's career.

Our goal is to explore the impact of Revelation's career in light of ecological concerns. While there are widely held beliefs and trends in the way medieval people viewed nature, there are also times when "works evince characteristics that bend or break" normal conventions and "point ahead" in a way that anticipates modern ecological concerns.[6]

1. THE TRIER APOCALYPSE

The Trier Apocalypse is a Latin version of the book of Revelation that has been corrected so it corresponds with Jerome's Vulgate, the standard version of the Bible in that time period.[7] While the Trier Apocalypse is from the ninth century CE, the details of its seventy-four watercolor illustrations suggest that it has roots in much earlier time periods.[8] The figures wear Roman style clothing; the furniture is antique for its period; its cities are towered; and the people read scrolls, not books. It also shows similarities to ornamental architecture from earlier periods.[9] These details suggest that this ninth-century manuscript is patterned on a much older original.

6. Christopher Clason, "'Gebrochen bluomen unde gras': Medieval Ecological Consciousness in Selected Poems by Walther von der Vogelweide," in *Rural Space in the Middle Ages and Early Modern Age: The Spatial Turn in Premodern Studies*, ed. Albrecht Classen (Berlin: Walter De Gruyter, 2012), 228.

7. See James Snyder, "The Reconstruction of an Early Christian Cycle of Illustrations for the Book of Revelation: The Trier Apocalypse," *Vigiliae Christianae* 18, no. 3 (1964): 148.

8. Richard Laufner et al., *Trierer Apokalypse: vollständige Faksimile—Ausg. im Orignalformat des Codex 31 der Stadtbibliothek Trier* (Graz: Akademische Druck-und Verlagsanstalt, 1974).

9. Snyder, "Reconstruction," 154–56.

The predecessors to the Trier Apocalypse could go back as far as the fourth to sixth centuries CE, making it a good place for us to start.

Trier's literalistic rendering of the images from Revelation typifies what will be true of most medieval illuminated Apocalypse manuscripts. A beast with seven heads is drawn as a beast with seven heads; earthquakes are represented by buildings that have gone to pieces like a dropped Lego set.[10] Because of this literalism, if we ask ecological questions of these illuminations, our answers emerge only through what is hinted at in the text of Revelation itself. Hail and blood fall from the sky, depicted as white or red dots. The seas teem with fish, first surrounding John on Patmos and later as the victims of blood, millstones, or mountains thrown into the sea.

One of the most striking images in the Trier apocalypse is its representation of the dragon's pursuit of the woman clothed with the sun:

> So when the dragon saw that he had been thrown down to the earth, he pursued the woman who had given birth to the male child. But the woman was given the two wings of the great eagle, so that she could fly from the serpent into the wilderness, to her place where she is nourished for a time, and times, and half a time. Then from his mouth the serpent poured water like a river after the woman, to sweep her away with the flood. But the earth came to the help of the woman; it opened its mouth and swallowed the river that the dragon had poured from his mouth. (Rev 12:13-16)

Almost all medieval manuscripts of Revelation choose to depict this scene of vivid action. In most cases, the water from the dragon disappears into a nondescript hole in the ground. In some cases, the water that pours from the dragon's mouth is not even directed at the woman.[11] In the Trier Apocalypse, however, the earth is personified with a head, upper torso, and open mouth, actively sucking the water away from the woman to protect her. This fits Trier's overall artistic

---

10. See folio 52 for a good example.

11. Note that in the Bamburg Apocalypse this story is rendered differently. Here the water does seem to be directed at the woman in a more threatening way. See Ernst Harnischfeger, *Die Bamberger Apokalypse* (Stuttgart: Urachhaus, 1981), folio 30.

program of a literal and episodic depiction of Revelation. Trier also personifies the four winds in its depiction of Revelation 7:1-3. The way the Trier Apocalypse personifies the earth attributes a unique agency to the earth itself. Why would the Trier Apocalypse present the earth like this? Understanding the environmental context of the early medieval period may provide some clues.

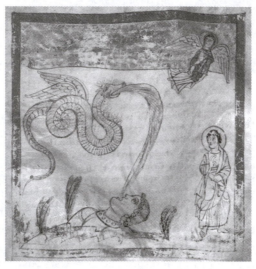

This illumination of Revelation 12:13-16 from the Trier Apocalypse shows the personification of the earth as it sucks up the water from the dragon intended to drown the woman clothed with the sun.

The period between 350 and 950 CE sees a general decline in classical culture (in other words, that which was inherited from Greece and Rome) and its relationship with the land. This period saw cultural failures and vulnerabilities of agricultural societies. There was, at the same general time, a "climatical anomaly" in which the average temperature was 1.5°c. cooler than normal.[12] Tree lines descended from mountains deeper into valleys. Fisheries once depleted by the Romans start to show signs of recovery. A Roman statesman, Cassiodorus (d. 575), reported a dry fog that occluded the sun for weeks, probably due to large-scale volcanic activity elsewhere on

12. Richard Hoffmann, *An Environmental History of Medieval Europe* (Cambridge: Cambridge University Press, 2014), 67.

the planet.[13] A combination of cultural and environmental affects changed people's relationship with the land. Fields were abandoned, fewer cereals grown, and livestock were grazed rather than stall-fed as wealthy Romans had done. Environmental historian Richard Hoffman describes the general situation as "sedentary agropasto-ralism." In the early medieval period (between the fifth and the eighth centuries), he says, we find "a renaturing, a decolonization, of western European landscapes" almost everywhere.[14]

Details of how medieval peoples depicted the natural world might "provide clues" as to how they "interpreted their interaction with the natural environment."[15] In the case of the Trier Apocalypse, it seems that Revelation might have helped its artist describe what he or she knew. The decolonization of nature, along with cultural decline, led to what Hoffman calls "fatalist attitudes."[16] Cold winters, famine, and epidemics were interpreted as God's punishment for sin. Despair at the material world led to a desire for an anticipated apocalypse. It is not hard to imagine Revelation as a generative component of such an experience of the natural world. Revelation expresses pessimism about human control and asserts suprahuman forces. A sense of a lack of control could have led to Trier's personification of the earth as an independent force. The artist's worldview does not see the earth, humans, and God as opposed to one another. The earth instead becomes an integral component of the opposition to the forces of evil. Revelation has not created antagonism toward the earth, but instead prompts contemplation of the connection between the earth, humans, and God. The artistic mind-set behind the Trier Apocalypse "used the natural world as one means to illuminate the human condition."[17]

13. We see the evidence for this in ice core data from Greenland and Antarctica. See ibid., 69.

14. Ibid., 66–67.

15. Connie Scarborough, ed. *Inscribing the Environment: Ecocritical Approaches to Medieval Spanish Literature* (Hawthorne, NY, and Berlin: Walter de Gruyter, 2013), 155.

16. Hoffmann, *Environmental History*, 55.

17. Ibid., 155. Scarborough here is not discussing Revelation or the Trier Apocalypse, but other literature of this time period.

2. THE BEATUS APOCALYPSE

The "Beatus Apocalypse" refers to a commentary on Revelation finished in 786 CE by a monk and priest named Beatus, accompanied by illuminations by an unnamed artist.[18] Beatus was from the Abbey of Santo Toribio at Liébana, nestled in a mountainous region in northern Spain. This was not a time and location of great apocalyptic fervor, so Beatus must have had some other impetus behind his interest in Revelation. Two primary factors seem to have spurred this manuscript.

First, Revelation endured much suspicion, just as it had in the early church. In 633 CE a council in Toledo (in central Spain) had to reassert the canonicity of Revelation. In order to give teeth to this pronouncement, the council ordered that Revelation be read at mass on Sundays between Easter and Pentecost. Such a move would have made people aware of Revelation in a new way. Second, Beatus was in theological battle with Christian "adoptionists." Adoptionists believed (heretically, according to Beatus) that Jesus was adopted as God's son at his baptism and was not eternally divine. Some of Beatus's commentary on Revelation is tailored to counter adoptionist theology. Thus, a combination of church promulgation, new liturgical use, and theological argument made Revelation a popular book in early medieval Spain.[19] This is the context in which we will situate Beatus's interpretation of Revelation and the images that accompanied it.

We do not have Beatus's original manuscript, but thirty-two copies of it have survived, a testament to its popularity and persistence in the following centuries. The pictures of Beatus are very closely linked with the textual commentary, which suggests collaboration between Beatus and the artist. Although each of the thirty-two surviving copies is unique, they share clear familial resemblance. Rather than try to examine all thirty-two of these manuscripts, we will focus on one, called the Morgan Beatus (M.644 in the Pierpont Morgan Library in

---

18. John Williams, *The Illustrated Beatus: A Corpus of Illustrations of the Commentary on the Apocalypse*, 5 vols. (London: Harvey Miller Publishers, 1994).

19. See the comment by Williams, *The Illustrated Beatus*, "Thus the Apocalypse by its nature, and the predominantly Tyconian Commentary by the historical circumstances which had produced it, were eminently suitable for revival versions of orthodoxy, in the context of heresy and persecutions" (1:114).

New York City).[20] Originating in approximately 922 CE, the Morgan Beatus is one of the earliest surviving Beatus manuscripts. It is also visually striking: the "chromatic brilliance and energy of its style is outstanding."[21] "Chromatic brilliance" means the Morgan Beatus has amazing colors. Its images pulse with deep hues, contrasts, and flamboyant patterns, which will help us understand its view of the natural world (see fig. 2).[22]

Nature is given florid colorization and detail throughout the manuscript. Mountains are depicted with overlapping shapes that look like boulders covered with green fronds. The call of the birds (Rev 19:17-18) gives the artist an opportunity to revel in the variety of nature. Many of the birds seem to be depicted accurately, with differing plumage, color patterns, and shapes. Beatus includes an interlude focused on Noah's ark, which he takes from a commentary written in the fourth century by Gregory, the Bishop of Elvira in southern Spain. This text interprets the ark allegorically, calling the ark an image of the church and Noah a prefiguration of Christ. Its placement, right after the letters to the seven churches (Rev 2–3), makes sense in this context. The ark here would symbolize the universal church as it navigates the world. The artist, however, ignores this allegorical interpretation. The depiction of Noah has no christological emphasis; he seems like an afterthought. The focus instead is on the "menagerie of beasts," which are not even alluded to in the text used by Beatus.[23] The animals (including giraffe, ape, serpents, and elephant) are rendered naturally. Their colors, however, are vividly unnatural: blue, yellow, red, and purple (see fig. 1). This suggests that, from the artist's point of view, creation is every bit a part of the drama of the Apocalypse as the church or humanity. The Morgan Beatus shows no evidence of an adversarial understanding of humanity's relationship with nature. On the contrary, the artist's interpretation

20. John Williams and Barbara A. Shailor, eds., *A Spanish Apocalypse: The Morgan Beatus Manuscript* (New York: George Braziller and Pierpont Morgan Library, 1991).

21. Williams and Shailor, *Illustrated Beatus*, 2:21.

22. In the case of the Morgan Beatus, we know the name of the artist. He includes a colophon in which he praises himself as the artist with an acrostic poem built on his name. See Williams and Shailor, *Illustrated Beatus*, 2:21.

23. Williams and Shailor, *A Spanish Apocalypse*, 179.

suggests that it is integral—a key component of God's revelation in the Apocalypse and indispensable to theological reflection.

Nature's indispensability is further evident in the Morgan Beatus's depiction of mountains. We have evidence from literary sources of the importance of wilderness and mountains in medieval Spain. The hagiographic tale *Vida de San Millán de la Cogolla* by Gonzalo de Berceo is a striking example. It tells the story of Millán, who goes into the mountains for ascetic reasons, where he lives like a hermit. While he encounters wild animals and snakes there, he is so strong spiritually that they do not bother him. In fact, the trees and mountains are blessed because of his presence.[24] The natural world is "omnipresent" in medieval Spain. It does not serve just as decoration, but had "intrinsic value for their originally intended audience."[25] Such a backdrop suggests taking a closer look at three different ways mountains function in the Morgan Beatus.

First, the Morgan Beatus makes mountains prominent. In Revelation 14:1-5 John sees a vision of the lamb standing on mount Zion, surrounded by the 144,000 faithful who have the name of God written on their foreheads. Beatus's depiction of this scene makes the mountain very prominent. The entire bottom panel is dedicated only to the mountain, which then extends up into the second tier with the lamb on top. The mountain dwarfs all other figures in the scene, even the lamb. Other manuscripts lack this emphasis. The mountain in the Trinity Apocalypse (thirteenth century), for instance, seems like an afterthought. It is barely visible behind a standing human figure. Beatus, in comparison, gives great value and prominent placement to the mountain (see fig. 3).

Second, Beatus introduces mountains into nonmountainous scenes in Revelation. Beatus's first extensive rendering of mountains comes in its depiction of Revelation 6:12-17, which narrates

24. Scarborough, *Inscribing the Environment*, 40–41.
25. Ibid., 149. See also Albrecht Classen, "The Discovery of the Mountain as an Epistemological Challenge: A Paradigm Shift in the Approach to Highly Elevated Nature. Petrarch's *Ascent to Mont Ventoux* and Emperor Maximilian's *Theuerdank*," in *The Book of Nature and Humanity*, ed. David Hawkes and Richard G. Newhauser (Turnhout: Brepols, 2013), 3–18. Classen shows the intricate interaction between mountains and people's physical environments, and their personal and theological imaginations.

those forced to flee and hide in the mountains. Here, the opening of the sixth seal brings an earthquake, darkened sun, and blood moon. The rich elites and rulers (6:15) run for the mountains as they cry: "Fall on us and hide us from the face of the one seated on the throne and from the wrath of the Lamb" (6:16). Beatus depicts three mountains at the bottom of the page inhabited by those who cried out. An image from later in the book depicts the attack of Gog and Magog (Rev 20:7-8) on people huddled in a church. At the bottom, the artist has recapitulated the mountains from chapter 6; they look almost identical.[26] The words superimposed over the image describe this bottom frame as "those who hid in the mountains." The inclusion of mountains here has no basis in Revelation 20; it is only "tenuously connected to either the Apocalypse or the Commentary" (see fig. 4).[27] The mountainous region from which Beatus originated was likely seen as an actual place of refuge, either from the invasions of the Visigoths in 711, or, later, the Muslims (756–788).[28] The artist's deep experience of the natural world wends its way into the interpretation of Revelation.

Third, Beatus makes a mountain part of the new Jerusalem at the end of time. Beatus uses two large images to depict the new Jerusalem from Revelation 21:1-27 (f. 222v and 223). The image on the left-hand side offers a macro-view of the city. On the right a more detailed image focuses on the river of life and the trees with fruit (22:1-5). In the bottom right corner of this focused image, John and his angel stand on a mountain, observing the city. This detail comes from Revelation 21:10, in which the angel takes John to a great mountain from which to view the city. The Morgan Beatus gives this mountain unusual prominence. Most manuscripts have the mountain physically outside the limits of the city, a distant vantage point from which John can see everything being revealed to him.[29] Such an interpretation is the plain sense of the text. In the Morgan

26. See Williams and Shailor, *A Spanish Apocalypse*, 207, who claim that this image is "modeled" on folio 151.

27. Ibid.

28. Ibid., 129–42.

29. The Trier, Trinity, and Douce Apocalypses all show the mountain as clearly external to the city, simply a vantage point from which the city can be viewed.

Beatus Apocalypse the mountain is within the city itself, depicted identically to other mountains in the manuscript (see fig. 6).[30] The prototype for the Beatus manuscripts originated in a very mountainous region of northern Spain. In such a context, we might not be surprised to see a mountain that persists in the midst of the newly created earth—a consistency between old and new. To recall language from our discussion of the future in chapter one, the Beatus artist here suggests that God will make "all things new," not make "all new things." Beatus intuits that there is continuity between the present natural environment and the new heaven and the new earth.

When we interrogate the Morgan Beatus with eco-critical questions, a striking legacy emerges. The details in no way support a primarily adversarial relationship with the natural world. Instead, we find a respect and love for their surroundings that shines through in these illuminations. We should not call the Beatus creators environmentalists, but there is a sense in which they have an "appreciation of the ecology and the esthetics of the natural world."[31] Connie Scarborough, in her discussion of medieval Spanish literature, claims that the "wilderness of the mountains figures prominently in the plot" of these tales.[32] The same could be said about Beatus. Mountains as a place of beauty, refuge, and eschatological hope contribute to the plot of Revelation. The "tangible reality" of their natural surroundings becomes constitutive in their artistic and theological constructions.[33] At the same time, Revelation provides a scriptural starting point for contemplation of the natural world.

3. GOTHIC MANUSCRIPTS
OF THE THIRTEENTH CENTURY

Unlike the Beatus manuscripts, which seemed not to be fueled by apocalyptic fervor, the opposite is the case in the thirteenth century.

30. This holds true for other Beatus manuscripts as well, such as the Silos Beatus: Manuel Moleiro et al., *Códice de Santo Domingo de Silos* (Barcelona: M. Moleiro, 2001).

31. Scarborough, *Inscribing the Environment*, 149. She is discussing other literature of this time period, not Revelation specifically.

32. Ibid., 42.

33. Ibid., 155.

Figure 1: Morgan Beatus (MS M.644 79r). Image of Noah and the ark from the Morgan Beatus manuscript. This image is not directly related to Revelation at all. Artist ignores christological importance of Noah as a prefiguration of Christ and focuses on the animals instead. The artist emphasizes a variety of animals and gives them vivid colors.

Figure 2: Morgan Beatus (MS M.644 109r). Image of "the altar [of] the souls of those who had been slaughtered for the word of God and for the testimony they had given" (Rev 6:9). The artist introduces birds as representations of the souls, and gives them the same vivid colors as the souls themselves in the lower portion of the image. Revelation 6:11 says they were given white robes, but that detail is not followed by the artist.

Figure 4: Morgan Beatus (MS M.644 215v). Image of the attack of Gog and Magog (Rev 20:7-10). This image shows, in its bottom register, people hiding in the mountains even though this is not mentioned in the text in Revelation 20. The artist has recapitulated the scene from Revelation 6:16, where people do hide in the mountains.

Figure 3: Morgan Beatus (MS M.644 174v). Image of the lamb on top of Mount Zion (Rev 14:1-5). The four living creatures are at the top. The mountain and its foliage are prominent here, dwarfing every other element of the scene.

Figure 6: Morgan Beatus (MS M.644 223r). Image of the New Jerusalem. Here the artist makes the mountain look as if it is part of the new city itself, even though the text makes it sound quite distant (Rev 21:10).

Figure 5: Morgan Beatus (MS M.644 220r). Image of the dead standing before the throne (which is in a separate image) and the sea giving up its dead (Rev 20:11-15). Those condemned to be thrown into the lake of fire are shown with drab clothing (cf. fig. 2, where the righteous have vibrant colors in their clothing).

Figure 7: *Saint John's Bible*. Image of the Four Horsemen from Revelation 6. The artist has given the scene a modern interpretation, suggesting that many of our modern-day plights are ecological in nature.

Figure 8: *Saint John's Bible*. Image of the New Jerusalem. This image combines imagery from many earlier parts of the Saint John's Bible. The small squares at the bottom represent humans, giving us a mission at the end and tempering an eschatology that could become uncomfortably too complete.

The career and writings of Joachim of Fiore (1135–1202) fanned the embers of apocalypticism. His work was influential for centuries and increased interest in Revelation.[34] Fiore described a world in apocalyptic turmoil, claimed that the antichrist had been born, and predicted that the world was rapidly approaching its end. Joachim's genius was his ability to coordinate the patterns of history with interpretation of the book of Revelation and other biblical prophecy. Moreover, ongoing conflict between Christians and Muslims in Eastern Europe and in the crusades were a "nurturing ground" for apocalypticism.[35] Europe's invasion by people with a different religion was interpreted as a sign of the end times.[36] Such fervor sets the backdrop for renewed interest in Revelation in France and England in the thirteenth century. Here we will focus on two manuscripts, the Trinity Apocalypse and the Douce Apocalypse, both from the thirteenth century.

The Trinity Apocalypse is a fully illuminated manuscript accompanied by the text of Revelation in French and an interpretation by a man named Berengaudus. We know very little of him; scholars do not even agree on when he lived.[37] His writing probably influenced Joachim of Fiore, so he helped revive an interpretation of Revelation that sought to give it a historical and literal interpretation. The Douce Apocalypse has two parts. The first part is a sparsely illustrated text and interpretation of Revelation in Anglo-Norman (it ends at Rev 17:8). The second part is a fully illuminated Latin Apocalypse, with selections from the commentary of Berengaudus.

The fact that both of these apocalypses were at least partially written in the vernacular (that is, the common language and not Latin) suggests that they were intended for private rather than liturgical

34. Bernard McGinn, *Visions of the End: Apocalyptic Traditions in the Middle Ages* (New York: Columbia University Press, 1979), 126–42.

35. Ibid., 149.

36. One example of this is the "Toledo Letter," a prophecy thought to have originated in Muslim circles. It employs a variety of phenomena, such as an eclipse, war, and discord—boilerplate elements of apocalyptic expectation inspired by Revelation—to predict the beginning of the end. See McGinn, *Visions of the End*, 152.

37. Derk Visser, *Apocalypse as Utopian Expectation (800–1500): The Apocalypse Commentary of Berengaudus of Ferrières and the Relationship between Exegesis, Liturgy, and Iconography* (Leiden: Brill, 1996).

use. Their size and imagery tie them to wealthy or royal families. The illuminated initial letter of the Douce Apocalypse, for example, shows a knight and a lady kneeling before the cross. They hold distinctive shields that connect them to Edward, son of Henry III and his wife, Eleanor of Castile, who were married in 1254.[38] Other images suggest that patrons with a courtly background commissioned the manuscript.

The thirteenth-century manuscripts show an increased emphasis on realism, especially compared with what we saw in Beatus. Faces look more human, buildings have realistic architectural detail, and soldiers have period armor. This level of detail extends also to the natural world. The Douce Apocalypse, for instance, is full of leafy foliage, often with accurate depictions of real leaves. This fits a broader trend of the time period. We have an example of similarly realistic foliage carved into the decoration of Rheims Cathedral from about 1240 CE. The Douce Apocalypse's rendering of the scene from Revelation 13, in which the nations worship the beast, devotes the entire top half of the illustration to maple and vine foliage.[39]

We can also see the tendency toward accuracy through the example of birds. In the Morgan Beatus the birds showed some variety, but the goal was not to depict them accurately or with their natural colors. In a manuscript like the Trinity Apocalypse, however, we see an early form of naturalism that depicts some of the birds as they are found in nature. In Revelation 19:17-21 an angel standing in the sun calls out for the birds:

> Come, gather for the great supper of God, to eat the flesh of kings, the flesh of captains, the flesh of the mighty, the flesh of horses and their riders—flesh of all, both free and slave, both small and great. (Rev 19:17-18)

38. Nigel J. Morgan, *The Douce Apocalypse: Picturing the End of the World in the Middle Ages* (Oxford: Bodleian Library, 2006), 9.

39. Peter K. Klein, ed., *Apokalypse, Ms. Douce 180* (Graz: Akademisch Druck- u. Verlagsanstalt, 1983), 49.

This illumination of Revelation 19:17-18 from the Trinity Apocalypse depicts the assembly of the birds as they prepare to eat the flesh of the powerful, called "the great supper of God." Used by permission of Master and Fellows of Trinity College Cambridge.

The text moves on to discuss the capture of the beast (19:20) and then concludes: "and all the birds were gorged with their flesh" (19:21). While this episode spans only a few verses, in the thirteenth-century manuscripts the illustrators almost always separate it into two images: first the call of the birds and then their feast.[40] Breaking this episode into two illuminations stems from its integral role in Revelation: these birds mark the beginning of the end of the end. The dual depiction also tells us something about the artist and interpretation: he or she wanted to depict more birds! In the Trinity Apocalypse the birds assemble as God's front line against the beast and his army. Several types of birds are easily identified: stork or crane, owl, and eagle. Two other birds are further singled out because of their color: a jay (blue stripes on the wing) and the magpie (black and white plumage). In the next scene, the actual feast of the birds, the magpie and jay are gone; it seems that only raptors, such as eagles, owls, and hawks, are left to consume the flesh.

40. The Lambeth Apocalypse (also thirteenth century) is a rare counter-example.

This illumination of Revelation 19:21 from the Trinity Apocalypse depicts the birds gorging on the flesh of the beast and his army as an angel prods them into hell. Used by permission of Master and Fellows of Trinity College Cambridge.

The Trinity Apocalypse's thirteenth-century context helps explain its natural interest, particularly birds. There is a rising interest in the natural world in this time period.[41] One medieval apocalypse manuscript from the thirteenth century, the Bremen Apocalypse, includes the Latin names adjacent to each bird in its depiction of Revelation 19:17-21. A book called The Bestiary, based on ancient Greek and Latin predecessors, had drawings of various animals and birds. Its goal was primarily moral, but it did contain some natural observations. Along with pictures and descriptions of the animals, the bestiary offered an allegorical interpretation of the animal's significance.[42] Some of the pictures of birds in the Trinity Apocalypse were probably based on drawings from a bestiary. On the other hand,

41. Albert the Great was a thirteenth-century Dominican friar from Germany whose work *De Animalibus* is seen by many as the first naturalistic and scientific work of the Middle Ages.

42. Christian Heck and Rémy Cordonnier, *The Grand Medieval Bestiary: Animals in Illuminated Manuscripts* (New York: Abbeville Press, 2012). See Willene Clark, "Zoology in the Medieval Latin Bestiary," in *Man and Nature in the Middle Ages*, ed. Robert G. Benson and Susan J. Ridyard (Sewanee, TN: University of the South Press, 1995), 223–38, for a discussion of the disagreements regarding the bestiary's relationship to later science (especially p. 224, n. 6).

some of the birds in the Trinity Apocalypse were likely drawn from personal experience.[43] We have evidence that cranes, peacocks, parrots, jays, magpies, and goldfinches were all held in captivity by rich elites, the very group who likely commissioned these manuscripts.[44] Captive birds likely provided models for the artists to follow.

The call of the birds from Revelation 19 also was an occasion for artists to be creative. Because these manuscripts were derived from one another, the scenes often coalesce into stable patterns.[45] The birds break this trend. The birds are almost always divided up into two scenes, but beyond that, we find variety in how the scenes are composed. For example, the Trinity, Getty, and Lambeth Apocalypses all depict this scene from Revelation 19 in unique ways. The idea was conventional but the execution was not. This suggests that, in the case of birds, Revelation was functioning as a point of embarkation for the artist to illustrate the natural world with freedom and creativity.[46]

One could imagine an artist wanting to create crazy, wild, ravenous birds, ones that would be in concert with other imagery in the book of Revelation. But this is not the trend in thirteenth-century Gothic manuscripts. Instead we find a persistence of the natural. In Revelation 12:16, the earth swallows up water from the dragon to protect the woman clothed with the sun. The natural world rises up to defend God's righteousness and the earth itself. Birds in these thirteenth-century manuscripts function quite similarly. The birds from Revelation

43. W. B. Yapp, *Birds in Medieval Manuscripts* (London: British Library, 1981), 71–75. The bestiaries themselves offered a "random mix of the factual and the imagined," so some accurate natural information could have been supplied by them (Clark, "Zoology," 235).

44. Yapp, *Birds*, 75. It is also likely that in the case of some birds, natural observation resulted in a description of its actual behavior (see Clark, "Zoology," 233–34).

45. Scholars go so far as to create family trees for these manuscripts, delineating which came first and who influenced whom. See, for instance, Nigel Morgan, *Illuminating the End of Time: The Getty Apocalypse Manuscript* (Los Angeles: The J. Paul Getty Museum, 2011), 13.

46. We do see this natural interest in illuminations of other manuscripts during this time, particularly the Psalter (see, for instance, the Ormesby Psalter or the DeLisle Psalter, both from the fourteenth century). In these other texts, however, the natural images were mostly ornamental, or worked in as part of an elaborate initial. Revelation is unique because the birds are part of the narration from the text itself.

19 refuse to let the forces of evil have the last word. They appear in the Trinity Apocalypse as a flock of resisters, pitiful next to an armor-clad army led by a seven-headed beast. In a Hitchcockesque scene, the raptors attack and pluck while others stand sentinel over the proceedings, shepherding the unrighteous and the beast into the open maw of hell.

II. The Saint John's Bible—A Modern Manuscript

Manuscripts became obsolete after the invention of the printing press in the fifteenth century. In the late 1990s, Saint John's Abbey and University in central Minnesota wanted to find a way to commemorate the coming millennium that would give glory to God and ignite the fires of artistic imagination.[47] Their idea was the Saint John's Bible, the first illuminated manuscript, with all of the art and writing done by hand, in five hundred years.

The Saint John's Bible was produced intentionally like past illuminated manuscripts using traditional paints, brushes, quills, and vellum. At the same time, it is a modern work. Most of its illuminations eschew the literal, episodic renderings of biblical scenes that we saw in the medieval manuscripts. Instead, various components of a text are combined into one image. This fits an overall "synchronic" and "condensed" style that is found in most time periods since the Reformation.[48] The art in the Saint John's Bible is also local and modern; its conveners wanted it to reflect their time and place. It utilizes modern biblical scholarship. It reflects a scientific understanding of the world (for example, prominent fossils in its illumination of Genesis 1). The flora and fauna used to illuminate and decorate come from the immediate ecological environment of Saint John's. The Saint John's Bible thus gives us a chance to jump to a very different time and place and explore Revelation's career through the same genre of illuminated manuscripts as those we explored from the medieval period. Because

---

47. Michael Patella, *Word and Image: The Hermeneutics of the Saint John's Bible* (Collegeville, MN: The Saint John's Bible, 2013), xi.

48. O'Hear and O'Hear, *Picturing the Apocalypse*, 285. They argue that this synchronic approach has interpretive advantages to a visionary text like Revelation because it concentrates and condenses interpretation into one scene.

of its less episodic, synchronic approach, the Saint John's Bible has far fewer illuminations of Revelation than the medieval manuscripts. Here we will focus on two: the four horsemen and the new Jerusalem.

The image of the four horsemen sits over the top of the text, tumbling down on either side. As a work of modern art, it bears little formal resemblance to the medieval manuscripts we have already discussed. The horses themselves are not prominent, solid swatches of color that gallop from left to right across the page. The lamb opens seals in the lower left. The scene is chaotic, replete with signs of war, violence, disease, and destruction. At the same time, a thin band of rainbow at the top offers a glimmer of hope.[49] Several aspects of this image intentionally engage environmental themes.

Donald Jackson, the sole artist for Revelation, interprets the four horsemen and their divinely ordained devastation in light of modern crises. The pale green horse (Rev 6:8) emits cancer, leprosy, and AIDS cells as they would look under a microscope. Modern cavalry, represented here as army tanks, encroach from the right. A significant component of the grim modern situation is given an environmental interpretation. Oil wells pump in the background. Bright yellow signs punctuate the design, warning of nuclear fallout. Revelation has not prompted a literal rendering of what the text says, but a reflection on how we understand the world's destruction today. On one hand, we succumb to disease—uncontrollable elements of the universe that destroy us. On the other hand, a thirst for oil and its geopolitical and environmental impacts are humanity's suicide—vast structures of self-wrought sin that destroy us. The complexities of modern society, especially its environmental elements, rise to the surface (see fig. 7).

The Saint John's Bible also disregards natural depiction at times. In the thirteenth-century manuscripts we saw a tendency toward the natural: the artists sought accuracy in their work. In its rendering of locusts, however, the Saint John's Bible leaves the text of Revelation, and nature itself, far behind. Revelation 9:1-11 describes a swarm of locusts that hardly look like locusts. They were equipped with armor, golden crowns, and lion's teeth. They had human faces and long

---

49. This rainbow recurs throughout the Saint John's Bible, representing God's new promises. See, for instance, the image of the new Jerusalem at the end of Revelation, which recapitulates the rainbow flamboyantly across the city.

hair, tails like a scorpion's, and scales like iron breastplates. The fifth trumpet looses them on the earth with the power to torment for five months. Such an assemblage of components often resulted in awkward renderings in medieval manuscripts.[50] When creating the Saint John's Bible, Donald Jackson did not think a locust was scary enough. To his sensibilities, a praying mantis was more menacing, so he used it as a model to replace the locust. Even then, the mantis did not seem to do justice to his interpretation of Revelation, so he made a mutant mantis, with exaggerated proportions. These mantises crawl around in the background of the image of the four horsemen and show up again individually on the next page. In this case, the artist, inspired by Revelation, left the text and natural world behind in order to create an adversary that satisfied the interpretive and theological appetite.

The Saint John's Bible also had to deal with Revelation's problematic eschatology. Donald Jackson's image of the new Jerusalem at the end of Revelation has many similarities to those in medieval manuscripts. The city is viewed from the top, with no attempt at three-dimensional architecture. The twelve gates are prominent and the scene is dominated by gold leaf. The image of God is not the lamb, as Revelation tells it, but is the shimmering white that recapitulates the Son of Man illumination from the book of Daniel. A prominent rainbow also ties together many illuminations from throughout this Bible and gives concrete expression to the hint of hope seen in the image of the four horsemen. The artistic rendering of the city emphatically ended Revelation and the entire Bible. When the committee that oversaw the project at Saint John's saw this image, they rejected it. God's new creation was so fully inaugurated that they saw no place for mission. There was not enough continuity between present and future. The committee longed to restart time so that humanity would be able to *do* something. Having time and space for mission or vocation is particularly important when giving Revelation an ecological interpretation. A fatalistic eschatology and flight from reality could make creation care unnecessary. Donald Jackson fixed the problem by sprinkling multicolored squares at the bottom of the page, meant to represent a sense of mission at the end—artistic homage to individual responsibility (see fig. 8). Just as the Morgan Beatus introduced a mountain into

---

50. See, for instance, the locusts in the Morgan Beatus (f. 140v).

the new city, the Saint John's Bible read the end of Revelation and asked: where are *we* in all of this? The final vision in the Saint John's Bible could be a call for an ecological vocation, one that emanates from God's making all things new.

III. Conclusion: "Environmental Entanglement"

What do we see of Revelation's career, based on having sampled several of its illuminated manuscripts? The results are mixed. Some of the art depicts graphically the destruction of the earth as described in Revelation. Such literal, episodic treatments offered visions of the heavens that could have led to hell for the earth.[51] The problem of eschatology that beset the early church also does not wane. Revelation's insistence on a new creation foists a question about the individual believer's place within a cosmic understanding of redemption and recreation.

On the other hand, these manuscripts reveal a Revelation that invites contemplation of the natural world and the place of humanity within it. Revelation seems not to inspire a flight from the natural world or reality. Instead it engenders contemplation, engagement, and interpretation of the relationship between text and environment. The medieval authors were not environmentalists but they do not abandon the world to its inexorable fate. The Saint John's Bible, in contrast, is consciously environmental. Although form and content are different, the competency of Revelation seems the same in both—prompting reflection at the nexus of text, humanity, and natural environment.

A certain school of cultural anthropology is fond of the term "entanglement." Entanglement is a way of theorizing how physical objects, landscapes, and surroundings impacted the evolution, development, and growth of the particularities of human culture.[52] There

51. This is a paraphrase of O'Hear and O'Hear, *Picturing the Apocalypse*, 291.
52. See, for example, the work of Christopher Y. Tilley, in which he discusses how rocks at various Neolithic sites in England invited a "creative" response from humans: *Interpreting Landscapes: Geologies, Topographies, Identities* (Walnut Creek, CA: Left Coast Press, 2009), 460. Also Ian Hodder's work that studies pottery and clay that demonstrates how entanglement is a "dialectic of dependence" between humans and things: *Entangled: An Archaeology of the Relationship between Humans and Things* (Malden, MA: Wiley-Blackwell, 2012), 206.

is, in other words, an inherent connection between how humans think and the environment in which they live. If we borrow this language, Revelation's career could be described as "environmental entanglement." The text and the environment cannot be discussed independently of each other; they are inextricably entangled. This entanglement reveals a natural environment that is worth contemplating and important in its own right. It is powerful and beautiful, a conversation partner with the text and its interpreters. Humanity and the natural world persist in the new creation. This suggests that Revelation's career does not prompt destruction and exploitation of the earth but instead promotes something deeper—a call to contemplate the entanglement among God, humans, creatures, and the future.

CHAPTER FIVE

Revelation's Legacy

Endings and Beginnings

"The end is just another place to start"
—The Okee Dokee Brothers

In an episode of the TV show "The Sopranos," the featured New Jersey Italian family is eating breakfast one morning. The son suggests that Christopher Columbus was an agent of genocide and imperialism. This sends his father, Tony, through the roof. Tony's Italian heritage and xenophobia produced anger at the suggestion that Columbus was anything other than a hero worthy of praise. To his son, who was being exposed to other ideas in school, Columbus's legacy was open for questioning. Was Columbus a hero or an agent of genocide? It might depend on whom you ask.

Legacies are tricky because they can be manipulated and can change like chameleons in different contexts. Revelation's ecological legacy is malleable. For those indifferent to the Christian tradition, Revelation will be deemed irrelevant. For those who want to know how we got where we are, and how we can change where we are headed, Revelation has insights and convictions that challenge the way we have lived, and continue to live, our lives. These challenges will prove particularly poignant in the ecological realm, as we have already seen in the first four chapters of this book.

The aim of this chapter is to harness Revelation's legacy in such a way that it gives us concrete ways to think about our environmental situation and what we can do about it. I am not an ecologist and I will not present specific plans of action. What I can do, however, is describe those scriptural insights—deemed to be revelatory by the church and the Christian community—that John of Patmos provides. Revelation offers a certain way of thinking about the problem, and some directions our actions ought to take, as we read a biblical text in light of our modern ecological situation. If read properly, we can craft a legacy for the book of Revelation that sets a course for proper environmental action.

I. Future Space and Action

The book of Revelation and our ecological crisis get us thinking about the future. While the specifics are different, they both tell a similar story: the planet is doomed. Revelation says that heaven and earth will pass away (21:1). Science says the same: in 7.6 billion years, the sun will reach its peak point as a red giant star, shining 3,000 times brighter than it does today and engulfing the earth.[1] Sometime later, the universe will in all likelihood collapse back in on itself, an inverse of the big bang that physicists refer to as the "big crunch."[2] A literal reading of Revelation and science agree that our planet's future is finite. Knowing these facts might lead to complacency. Since we know our future, ought we just to sit back and wait for the inevitable end?

Pope Francis, in his encyclical on the environment *Laudato Si'*, seems worried that eschatology leads to inaction. The encyclical is generally devoid of eschatology, although he does briefly discuss the ending of the book of Revelation. He quotes Revelation's words about how God will make all things new (21:5), a future in which

---

1. David Appell, "The Sun Will Eventually Engulf Earth—Maybe," *Scientific American* (September 2008). Accessed online July 20, 2016. http://www.scientificamerican.com/article/the-sun-will-eventually-engulf-earth-maybe.

2. Mary-Jane Rubenstein, *Worlds without End: The Many Lives of the Multiverse* (New York: Columbia University Press, 2014), 15 and 148–49.

eternal life will be what Francis calls a "shared experience of awe" (LS 243).[3] Though it is the end of the Bible, Francis is unwilling to let Revelation and its eschatology have the last word. He adds one more section, which starts: "*In the meantime*, we come together to take charge of this home which has been entrusted to us" (LS 244, italics added). Francis leaves the eschatology behind in order to call for action.

Eschatology and action need not be divorced from one another. Responding to Revelation's eschatology with inaction would be to misread it. The eschatology in the book of Revelation can actually provide a robust call for action in the ecological realm. Such a conclusion, however, may not be obvious from a cursory reading of the ending of Revelation. Building upon our work in previous chapters, we are situated to be able to make an argument for how Revelation's eschatology includes a call for radical action.

1. SPATIAL, NOT CHRONOLOGICAL, ESCHATOLOGY

Revelation's eschatology is too often understood as chronological, that it describes what will happen as events unfold in the future. This is why Pope Francis starts his final section with the phrase "in the meantime. . ." It sets a chronological distinction between now and the future. Following the lead of theologian Kathryn Tanner, we would do better to think of the future in terms that are spatial, not chronological. Eternal life is something *in* which Christians presently live, not some place they *will be*. Life in God is "not especially associated with any particular moment of time (past, present, or future)."[4] Because of this, the physical future of the world is irrelevant to the theological reality of a Christian eschatology. Our claims to eternal life transcend chronology and time itself. It is a life *in* God: "Since there may come a time when the world no longer exists, this placement in God cannot be equated with God's presence or

---

3. Pope Francis, *Laudato Si': On Care for Our Common Home* (Vatican City: Libreria Editrice Vaticana, 2015).

4. Kathryn Tanner, "Eschatology without a Future?" in *The End of the World and the Ends of God: Science and Theology on Eschatology*, ed. John Polkinghorne and Michael Welker, (Harrisburg, PA: Trinity Press International, 2000), 230.

placement within the world."[5] This means that despite what science tells us about the fate of the planet and cosmos, and despite what a literal interpretation of Revelation says will happen in the future, our hope for the future is not dependent upon a certain string of chronological events.

The way Tanner reorients the discussion of eschatology leads to the observation that John of Patmos spends a lot more time describing the spatial aspects of his visions than any temporal specifications as to when they will happen. John's visions are set vaguely in the future, but outside of the reference to a one-thousand-year period (20:4-10), John's visions focus on what things look like and what happens. He describes landscapes and events and generally avoids timetables.[6] The future in Revelation is a space, a kingdom that cannot coexist with the human empire as it exists on earth. Like Harry Potter and Voldemort, "neither can live while the other survives."[7] As Tanner says, "eternal life exists now in competition with another potentially all-embracing structure or pattern of existence marked by futility and hopelessness—the realm of death, in the broadest biblical sense."[8] The violence, conflict, and destruction in the book of Revelation—including that meted out on the planet and cosmos—is a result of the incompatibility of the realm of life with the realm of death. The apostle Paul sees this conflict when he says that all of creation is groaning, longing for liberation (Rom 8:18-25). The ultimate spatial configuration in the book of Revelation is one in which God dwells fully with humans. What was inaugurated in creation and recapitulated in the incarnation is fully consummated when "God himself will be with them" (Rev 21:3).

Once we see the spatial component of Revelation's eschatology, and how that space is in competition with space of the world, the need for action emerges. The eschatology of Revelation implores us to live in a way that rejects the dominant paradigms of empire. John

---

5. Ibid.

6. This is in contrast to some other ancient apocalyptic works that are much more interested in temporal speculation and specification. See, for instance, Daniel 9:24-27.

7. J. K. Rowling, *Harry Potter and the Deathly Hallows* (Scholastic, 2007), 429.

8. Tanner, "Eschatology," 230–31.

makes clear that those who act incorrectly, the cowards, faithless, polluted, murderers, idolaters, and so forth, will be thrown into the lake of fire (21:8). Actions will be judged, and certain human actions are required of us. The disposition of God ought to provide the model on which proper human action is based. God brings life, peace, and consolation (Rev 21:3-4). Those in need have their needs met: "to the thirsty I will give water as a gift from the spring of the water of life" (Rev 21:6). Tanner's exploration of Christian eschatology also finds the need for action. Her words seem entirely appropriate to the end of Revelation:

> Action is the proper response to take with respect to a world that is not the way it should be, because, although human action does not bring about life in God (that is God's unconditional gift to us), human action of a certain sort is what life in God requires of us. Only one way of living in this world—living so as to counter suffering, oppression, and division—corresponds to life in God, achieved in Christ. Life in God is not inactive then. Life in God sets a task for us.[9]

The ending of Revelation certainly provides hope, intended as it was for the oppressed and suffering in its Roman context. This hope, however, is not escapist. It sets a task for us. Revelation tells us that the powers will fall, indeed that the working of their downfall has begun. This should be a call for engagement in that process, for endurance, for living in such a way that rejects these powers. As Richard Bauckham states in his assessment of the theology of Jürgen Moltmann, "believers are liberated from accommodation to the *status quo* and set critically against it. . . . By arousing *active* hope the promise creates anticipations of the future kingdom within history."[10]

Revelation's vision of the future world rejects actions, no matter how big or small, that negatively impact the most vulnerable. Proper action will provide consolation, nourishment, and peace. An ecological reading of the eschatology of Revelation should cause us to rethink the myriad decisions we make each day and their environ-

9. Ibid., 234.
10. Richard Bauckham, *Theology of Jürgen Moltmann* (London: T&T Clark, 1995), 10.

mental impact. The book of Revelation calls us to be set critically against the status quo. This is Revelation's environmental legacy, to spur its readers to reject modes of living that harm the earth. This is not work that we do "in the meantime," because the future is now.

II. Environmental Entanglement and Integral Ecology

In chapter four we discussed Revelation's career by asking: how has it been read across the centuries? Our exploration of illuminated manuscripts suggested that the book did not necessarily prod people to destroy the earth, even though it depicts so much destruction. Instead, Revelation prompted contemplation of the natural world and the integration of the natural environment—whether birds, mountains, or oil wells—into the understanding of the Apocalypse. I called this "environmental entanglement," a phrase meant to express the way in which Revelation calls us to contemplate the world around us and to come to grips with the way all things are connected. God, humans, and creation are all entangled together.

Western society has historically separated humans from the natural world. Wild places needed to be conquered or were thought to be rife with danger. The Bible often emphasizes these exact ideas. The wilderness was seen as a place not suitable to agriculture, where no humans would go unless they were forced to. From the point of view of subsistence farmers, those who eked out an existence from the land, such an adversarial view might make sense. But it also led to the idea that "forest and especially wilderness were uninhabited, inhospitable and even threatening to humans."[11] Similar ideas persist throughout the history of the Christian tradition. In *Beowulf*, for example, the hero must kill Grendel and his mother, monsters of nature. Such a story fits into a larger pattern of *contemptus mundi* (contempt for the world), which creates an adversarial relationship

---

11. Richard Bauckham, *The Bible and Ecology: Rediscovering the Community of Creation* (Waco, TX: Baylor University Press, 2010), 111. Bauckham also points out that the Old Testament occasionally appreciates and has unique knowledge of the wilderness; see especially pp. 113–15.

between human and the environment, and also justifies any violence done against that environment.[12]

The Disney movie *Swiss Family Robinson* epitomizes *contemptus mundi*. In this movie, from 1960, a family is marooned on an unknown island after a shipwreck. The premise of the movie rests upon the danger of unknown nature, which teems with tigers, snakes, and other enemies. Although I remember this movie fondly from my childhood, watching it in the twenty-first century I found its depiction of the natural world appalling. Nature is there to be conquered and exploited in order to create the luxuries of civilization. Elephants and zebras are trapped, domesticated, and used as work animals to help them build. A huge snake attacks from a lake, leading to a classic human-versus-nature showdown. This movie represents the ideas that have plagued the natural world since humanity's beginning—a contempt for nature and a total disregard for its own integrity and the working of ecosystems.

In our modern situation, we have myriad things that impede our ability to contemplate the natural world. One of my kids was recently given a telescope for Christmas. We took it out in the front yard on a freezing cold and clear night to try to see the stars. We live in a city of about 100,000 people and the light pollution was so bad we could see nothing. Light pollution does not just impede my rudimentary attempts at astronomy. It disrupts bird migrations and causes problems for plant phenology.[13]

Increasing urbanization destroys habitats and removes humanity farther from the natural world. The only animals my family sees on a regular basis are squirrels, chipmunks, and annoying neighborhood dogs. It is a monumental event when a raccoon wanders up from the creek and makes a cameo in our backyard. It takes time, effort, and money to have any sort of opportunity to contemplate and be familiar with the natural world. We have to make a point to go

12. Richard Hoffmann, *An Environmental History of Medieval Europe* (Cambridge: Cambridge University Press, 2014), 96.

13. Travis Longcore and Catherine Rich, "Ecological Light Pollution," *Frontiers in Ecology and the Environment* 2, no. 4 (2004): 191–98; Richard H. Constant et al., "Light Pollution Is Associated with Earlier Tree Budburst across the United Kingdom," *Proceedings of the Royal Society B (Biological Sciences)* 283 (2016): 20160813.

camping in remote areas, which requires equipment, ample vacation time, and disposable income to pay for the excursion. For the urban poor, the chasm between daily life and wild, natural ecosystems is almost insurmountable.

Many cities do the best they can to make natural spaces. Parks can offer some semblance of an outdoor experience, but they generally do not provide a chance to see the breadth and depth of the interrelatedness of thousands of organisms as they have evolved. My university has an area of prairie restoration, planted with indigenous species. Places like this and city parks are helpful, but they are little more than paintings on a wall. They decorate and punctuate urban monotony, but they usually do not provide a chance to observe a real ecosystem.

Technology creates another barrier between individuals, communities, and ecosystems. John Ehrenfeld refers to technology as "a way of holding the world." It is one of the categories of our culture and one of the "filters through which we construct meaning."[14] Technology has a great capacity to help humanity in the world, but it also has a dark side. The problem is that technology has become "the primary means of obtaining human satisfaction," which has a "perverse effect on humanity."[15] Although the desire for technology often starts with a good intention, it eventually erodes our ability to be authentically human and impedes our ability to experience the natural world.

Every summer, my family rents a few rustic cabins on the north shore of Lake Superior. This past year I told myself: "I'm shutting my phone off and not looking at it all week." You can guess how well that went. It started with wanting to check the weather forecast—an innocuous need. Then I checked baseball scores and political polls. News articles and emails followed. Of course I needed to document how many steps I took on a hike. A beautiful sunrise set my mind racing to craft the perfect Facebook status update. When I shut the phone off and put it in the dresser, it whispered to me, like the ring

14. John R. Ehrenfeld, *Sustainability by Design: A Subversive Strategy for Transforming our Consumer Culture* (New Haven, CT: Yale University Press, 2009), 29.
15. Ibid., 29.

hanging around Frodo's neck. I exemplified what Erich Fromm calls our species' switch from a "being" mode of life to a "having" mode of life.[16] Such a modern way of being, of striving for technological satisfaction, "stifles the noninstrumental, transcendent characteristics of what it is to be human."[17] Technology threatens to strip away our human dignity by yielding to a form of "addiction to instrumentality—a machinelike existence—and to its relative, consumption."[18] Our separation from the natural world is a symptom of a deeper problem, but also a problem itself.

Rather than be adversarial and separate, we need to see how we are integrated with the world around us. Christiana Peppard, in her book *Just Water*, describes the way in which we are connected with our environment. Writing specifically about water, she observes that "our porous bodies mediate the world. . . . Through mouth and skin, we siphon the world in . . . we are embodied and in relationship. We are, literally and materially, shaped by our contexts."[19] John of Patmos, in a certain sense, would agree. John was a keen observer. He made repeated references to the stars, the sun, the moon, to animals and plants. He insists that the entirety of the cosmos is integrated into God's salvation. Humans, plants, animals, mountains, and stars are all in this together. While John's outlook is not ecological, the summit of his Apocalypse is one of interrelatedness:

> See, the home of God is among mortals.
> He will dwell with them;
> they will be his peoples,
> and God himself will be with them. (Rev 21:3)

We might consider this an integral theology. God and humans are meant to dwell interconnectedly. Such ideas fit nicely with an "integral ecology," described by Pope Francis as examining how "everything

---

16. Erich Fromm, *To Have or To Be?* (London: Bloomsbury Academic, 2013). Also quoted by Ehrenfeld, *Sustainability by Design*, 29.

17. Ehrenfeld, *Sustainability by Design*, 30.

18. Ibid.

19. Christiana Z. Peppard, *Just Water: Theology, Ethics, and the Global Water Crisis* (Maryknoll, NY: Orbis Books, 2014), 15.

is interconnected" (LS 138). The more we learn about the world, the more we realize that even things that seem disparate must be understood in relation to one another: "living species are part of a network which we will never fully explore and understand" (LS 138).

From these observations flows an ecological implication, that God's decision to dwell with humanity models a certain disposition that extends to all creation. We ought to dwell in close relationship with all of creation as well. John's eschatology offers a vision of the force that draws all things together. God's presence in this new dwelling situation is one of healing, caring, and consoling. Integral theology and ecology ought to adopt the same disposition toward all those things with which we are integrated. Exploitation and destruction have no place in this future.

A true integration of humans with nature—an integral ecology—will take us into the "heart of what it is to be human" (LS 11). Pope Francis points to his namesake, Francis of Assisi, as someone who understood deeply the connection between humans and their natural environment. All creatures were united with the "bonds of affection" (LS 11). While such words might be ignored or dismissed as just some naïve romantic words about nature, Pope Francis suggests that this is not the case. Deep love and affection will affect "the choices which determine our behavior . . . if we feel intimately united with all that exists, then sobriety and care will well up spontaneously" (LS 11).

Talking about love and affection for the natural world, it might seem we have left the book of Revelation far behind, with its manifold destruction of the earth and its flora and fauna. We have seen, however, that John himself was responding to the earth's destruction that he inherited and experienced, not calling for it anew. At the same time, the art from illuminated manuscripts has used Revelation as a point of embarkation to contemplate the natural world, not necessarily to engage in its destruction. The book of Revelation implores us to contemplate the ways in which all of creation is bound up with the same destiny. God is our common creator and we are all in this together. An apocalyptic ecology is one that recognizes this connection, the way in which we siphon the world in and how the world metabolizes in us. The world is a "joyful mystery to be contemplated" (LS 12).

III. Ecological Alternative and Deep Ecology

In chapter two we explored the perspective of the Book of Watchers and how it responded to war and destruction by offering an ecological alternative. It envisions a future without human civilization, marked by vast wild spaces. The eschatology of Revelation, by contrast, is urban. While these are drastically different visions, they share a core method in which God provides an ecological alternative to the status quo.

In a way, these perspectives from apocalyptic literature mirror the deep ecology movement. Both see the need for a drastic break between the way the world currently operates and how it needs to operate in the future. Deep ecology, founded by Arne Naess, attempts to shift the view of the environmentalist movement from one that is anthropocentric (focused on the needs of humans), to biocentric (focused on the needs and rights of all life forms).[20] The flourishing of nonhuman life forms has inherent value that is not derived just from its utility to humanity. Biodiversity is also inherently valuable on its own terms. Humans have no right to reduce or impede the flourishing of nonhuman life forms on the planet. One can see the types of policies that might follow from signing on to the perspectives of deep ecology: wilderness should not just be protected and managed, but should be untouched by humanity.

There are ways in which the deep ecology movement could be critiqued. Some have cast it as imperialistic, a quintessentially American endeavor (despite the fact that its founder was Norwegian). At times, the agenda of deep ecology is imposed on another country without taking into account the needs of the local population.[21] There are also environmental problems that impinge more directly and imminently on the lives of the poor, such as water quality, erosion, and air

20. Arne Naess, "The Shallow and the Deep, Long-range Ecology Movement: A Summary," *Inquiry* 16 (1973): 95–100. See his more recent "The Basics of Deep Ecology," *Trumpeter* 21 (2005): 61–71.

21. Ramachandra Guha, "Radical American Environmentalism and Wilderness Preservation: A Third World Critique," *Environmental Ethics* 11 (1989): 71–83.

pollution.[22] It is easy for Americans to prioritize land conservation and wilderness preservation because we have so much land. Not all countries are so fortunate. Also, the total removal of humans from ecological goals can lead to problems and might be unrealistic. The tension here lies between anthropocentric and biocentric forms of environmentalism.

To the extent that there is a debate between biocentric and anthropocentric ecological movements, perhaps an apocalyptic ecology can provide a different way forward. The "ecological alternative" in *1 Enoch* and Revelation is primarily *theo*centric.[23] It starts neither with humanity, nor with life in general, but with God and God's role as creator. From God and the goodness of creation flow the critiques of deviations from proper care for that creation.[24] A theocentric ecology expresses a cosmic sense of the common good, a place from which all things and creatures find their proper value in the broad scope of God's creation.[25] Lest we usurp the role of God, Pope Francis suggests that a good ecological ethic must start with God at its center:

> A spirituality which forgets God as all-powerful and Creator is not acceptable. That is how we end up worshipping earthly powers, or ourselves usurping the place of God, even to the point of claiming an unlimited right to trample his creation underfoot. The best way to restore men and women to their rightful place, putting an end to their claim to absolute dominion over the earth, is to

22. Ibid., 3; See also John F. Morton, "The Impact of Climate Change on Smallholder and Subsistence Agriculture," *Proceedings of the National Academy of Sciences* 104 (2007): 19680–19685.

23. I am far from the first to propose this idea in an ecological and theological context. See L. J. Van den Brom, "The Art of a 'Theo-Ecological' Interpretation," *Nederlands Theologisch Tijdschrift* 51 (1997): 298–314. See also Ronald A. Simkins and John J. O'Keefe, "The Greening of the Papacy," *Journal of Religion and Society Supplement Series* 9 (2013): 5–15.

24. Some have rejected the idea of a theocentric ecological starting point. See Jan Deckers, "Christianity and Ecological Ethics: The Significance of Process Thought and a Panexperientialist Critique of Strong Anthropocentrism," *Ecotheology: Journal of Religion, Nature and the Environment* 9 (2004): 359–87.

25. See the similar idea in Simkins and O'Keefe, "The Greening of the Papacy," 13.

speak once more of the figure of a father who creates and who alone owns the world. Otherwise, human beings will always try to impose their own laws and interests on reality. (LS 75)

Francis here is talking about a new starting point in an ecological vocation.

We see hints of such an ecological vocation in John's Apocalypse. Four living creatures punctuate Revelation. They are the first things described that worship around the throne of God.

> Around the throne, and on each side of the throne, are four living creatures, full of eyes in front and behind: the first living creature like a lion, the second living creature like an ox, the third living creature with a face like a human face, and the fourth living creature like a flying eagle. And the four living creatures, each of them with six wings, are full of eyes all around and inside. Day and night without ceasing they sing,
>   "Holy, holy, holy,
>   The Lord God the Almighty,
>   who was and is and is to come." (Rev 4:6-8)

The details of these creatures symbolize all of creation. The lion is a wild animal, the ox a domesticated one; both are terrestrial. The eagle flies, the others do not. One is like a human. The creatures represent types of biological life from various domains.[26] Their eyes cover their entire inside and outside (4:8), making them introspective sentinels. These creatures are the vanguards in offering praise to God. The twenty-four elders follow their lead, casting their crowns before the throne and singing praises. Thus, in this first extended vision in the book of Revelation, we see the integral role that animals and all of creation play. In a decidedly "non-anthropocentric" turn, the animals first, and then the humans, train their gaze on the holy one. Richard Bauckham points out that the "human has no privilege

---

26. This observation is also made by Richard Bauckham, *Living with Other Creatures: Green Exegesis and Theology* (Waco, TX: Baylor University Press, 2011), who says that they are "representatives of creation" and of the entire "world of earthly creatures" (176–77).

or precedence here," which puts the focus on God instead.[27] The universe is theocentric, perceived most thoroughly by the omnivident creatures around the throne.

This is the true heart of John's conviction in the book of Revelation: the goodness of creation and all its creatures. The problem, as we have seen in earlier chapters, is that things have gone off the rails. John critiques his context because the powers of his age traded worship of the true creator for worship of a pretender. Rome's claims to control the universe confront John's monotheistic faith. When we see John's visions of what this proper worship looks like, animals lead the way in proper worship of God and stand sentinel around the throne.

John is not out on a limb in suggesting creation's role in praising God. Many psalms offer a similar idea, even if the imagery is less bizarre (such as Pss 148, 150). He offers, however, a way of viewing the world at odds with how humans have generally operated. Rather than follow the lead of nonhuman creation in praising God, we tend to eschew their example in pursuit of our own economic gain. John's vision, with animals first, is an ecological alternative to how we have structured our world today.

IV. Economic Lust and Ecological Debt

In Revelation, John critiques inequality between rich and poor. He lauds churches in the opening chapters for being poor (2:9), and denigrates those that are materially rich (3:17). He mocks the economic structures of the Roman Empire and claims that they are of Satan (13:11-18). A final lament makes fun of the excess and luxuries of the Roman elites (18:1-23). Finally, the new Jerusalem, which descends to the new earth, offers a way of providing for people that has no resemblance to normal human economics—food and water are provided freely to all. John observes, consciously in line with Israel's prophets before him (Rev 1:3), that empire skews toward the wealthy while the poor are oppressed, taken advantage of, and disenfranchised.

27. Ibid., 183.

In economic terms, the world does not look all that different today. The disparity between rich and poor has never been greater and continues to grow. The world economic forum 2014 global risk report lists "severe income disparity" as one of the top pressing global concerns. The top 358 billionaires worldwide are worth the combined income of the bottom 2.5 billion people (45 percent of the entire population of the earth).[28] Poor countries are crippled with debt, forced to pay 100 to 200 percent of their gross domestic product on interest alone, often more than they spend on education or healthcare.[29] Globally speaking, this puts most people in the United States among the very rich.

The disparity between rich and poor, both globally and within the United States, has a particularly environmental component. Problems from climate change, for example, are felt more acutely by the global poor. The influence of climate change will in part be determined by concurrent economic and social conditions and the extent to which these conditions make people resilient or vulnerable.[30] For example, changing climate will have an unbalanced impact on smallholder farms and those who practice subsistence agriculture.[31] Poor countries do not have the infrastructure or income to deal with rising seas, air pollution, or water pollution. By 2025, it is estimated that 5 billion people, out of a total global population of 8 billion, will experience water stress.[32] The statistics tumble into our newspapers and magazines pell-mell, becoming hard to fathom. The point, however, is that there is a connection between economics and ecology. We cannot separate the two. As Pope Francis says, "a true ecological approach *always* becomes a social approach; it must integrate questions of justice in debates on the environment, so as to hear *both the cry of the earth and the cry of the poor*" (LS 49).

28. Martin Donohoe, "Causes and Health Consequences of Environmental Degradation and Social Injustice," *Social Science and Medicine* 56, no. 3 (2003): 578.

29. Ibid., 579.

30. Karen L. O'Brien and Robin M. Leichenko, "Double Exposure: Assessing the Impacts of Climate Change within the Context of Economic Globalization," *Global Environmental Change* 10, no. 3 (2000): 225.

31. See Morton, "Impact of Climate Change."

32. Nigel W. Arnell, "Climate Change and Global Water Resources," *Global Environmental Change* 9 (1999): 31–49.

It is not easy to see the connection between economics and environment. Our society and our privilege occlude the impact of our actions. The structure of our world has "diminished the ability to know the consequences of actions taken by individuals or by collective social entities, because those consequences are often displaced in time and space, and as such have made responsibility problematic."[33] We may not think we are responsible, we may not feel responsible, but we need to think about the ways in which we are.

Almost sixty years ago, John Kenneth Galbraith pinpointed the root of the economic and environmental problem: a "gargantuan and growing appetite." He perceived that we must address the root cause: "Surely [the appetite] is the ultimate source of the problem. If it continues its geometric course, will it not one day have to be restrained? . . . It is as though, in the discussion of the change for avoiding automobile accidents, we agree not to make any mention of speed."[34] More recent treatments of the problem have seen the same connection: "resource degradation is simply the result of humankind's insatiable desire to produce and consume, leading to willful short-term greed and corruption with no heed for the future."[35] Our current ecological crisis is an extension of the very same economic crisis perceived by John of Patmos two thousand years ago—a system in which the rich and powerful consume obscene amounts and the vast number of poor struggle to survive. Both the poor and the earth cry out in woe because of what is being done to them.

One of the key insights that John can help us with is to see that the problem—both economic and environmental—is structural. Evil is not simply the aggregate of small things that we do wrong. Too often our solutions are little more than a "Band-Aid that masks deeper, cultural roots of our sustainability challenge."[36] Evil has been bred into the very structures of our society. In John's Roman

33. Ehrenfeld, *Sustainability by Design*, 60.

34. John Kenneth Galbraith, "How Much Should a Country Consume?" in *Perspectives on Conservation: Essays on America's Natural Resources*, Henry Jarrett, ed. (Baltimore, MD: Johns Hopkins University Press, 1958), 92.

35. B. H. Walker and David Salt, *Resilience Thinking: Sustaining Ecosystems and People in a Changing World* (Washington, DC: Island Press, 2006), 4–5.

36. John R. Ehrenfeld and Andrew J. Hoffman, *Flourishing: A Frank Conversation about Sustainability* (Stanford, CA: Stanford Business Books, 2013), 1.

context, he saw evil behind everything, especially Roman claims to control of the cosmos and their economic system based on obscene consumption and luxury. In a literal sense, the way John's book solves the problem is with the entire dismantling of a civilization—indeed a whole world—and a completely new creation. Profiling the drastic nature of John's remedy helps us understand the depth of his critique. If we don't get the diagnosis right to begin with—that the problem is structural—then we will never have the correct course of treatment.

Recognizing a structural problem has led some ethicists to talk about how the first world is in "ecological debt" to the third world. Ecological debt can be defined as "the debt accumulated by Northern, industrial countries toward Third-World countries on account of resource plundering, environmental damages and free occupation of environmental space, to deposit wastes, such as greenhouse gases, from the industrial countries."[37] This may seem unfair, but it is not. Those who live most of their lives in heated and air-conditioned suburban homes, commuting to and from work in comfortable cars, do not have the direct experience to know the extent of this ecological debt. It may be that middle-class families in industrial societies have never once made a conscious decision to pollute or oppress the global poor. But if the problem is structural, then those at the top, globally speaking, are responsible.

The structure of our economy and its ecological impact is not inevitable. It is not that we should not have an economic system, but the entire root and basis of our current system ought to be rethought. Our response cannot be simply a series of partial responses to pressing problems such as pollution or climate change. Pope Francis is instructive in calling instead for a new "distinctive way of looking at things, a way of thinking, policies, an educational program, a lifestyle, and a spirituality which together generate resistance to the assault of" today's status quo (LS 111). Why does profit have to be the bottom line? Why does anthropocentrism need to be a destructive assumption in our religion? Ethicist Cynthia

---

37. Cynthia Moe-Lobeda, *Resisting Structural Evil: Love as Ecological-Economic Vocation* (Minneapolis: Fortress Press, 2013), 207–8. Moe-Lobeda here is quoting from Acción Ecológica, a civil organization in Ecuador.

Moe-Lobeda offers three overarching reorientations for corporate policy that could help us reorient our economy in a way that would not be detrimental to the environment:

1. Replacing the financial bottom line with a triple bottom line of ecological sustainability, financial viability, and social impact;
2. Internalizing social and ecological costs that currently are externalized. (She offers the example of a corporation including the cost of keeping water clean, replacing cropland, and maintaining carbon neutrality as part of corporate calculations);
3. Measuring profit and loss not only by the quarter, but by the long-term future.[38]

I add here three points of conviction and action spurred by the book of Revelation that correlate with Moe-Lobeda's reorientation:

1. *Belief in and centrality of God as the creator and the interconnectedness of all life because of creation.* If our society truly took this seriously, its economic and ecological impact would be swift and deep. We would need to eliminate the gargantuan appetite that controls our structures and establish an entirely new way of thinking. Our most cherished and protected things, particularly the financial bottom line, would have a new foundation in God and an understanding of integral ecology.
2. *The courage to stand up to the machinations of empire and refuse to live by its assumptions and social and religious realities.* Few leaders today have the courage to envision real change; there is no one to follow. Who will raise serious ethical questions about ecological cost at a board meeting? Who will question corporate assumptions when policies are made? Who will suggest that a company's carbon footprint be part of its bottom line? Could a political candidate speak hard truths about the need for ecological change? We cannot pretend that solutions to the ecological crisis will emerge without anyone changing how they live. True solutions require a prophetic level of boldness because they will proffer significant structural change. They cannot just be strategies that make for "green" marketing.

38. Ibid., 203.

3. *A different pattern of thinking when it comes to the future.* John envisions a near complete break from the current world and the future world. His future world is economically and environmentally unrecognizable to us. If we cannot stop thinking about the next financial quarter, or the next election cycle, we are ecologically doomed. An apocalyptic ecology will expand the timeframe of reference and think long term instead. At the same time, that long-term thinking will envision a world that is radically different from the one in which we currently live.

Water provides a helpful test case. Christiana Peppard, in her book *Just Water*, offers a robust assessment of the world's water crisis in light of Roman Catholic social teaching. Water can be commodified in a way that is detrimental to both the environment and the poor. Water is a "profitable substance" in the twenty-first century, sometimes more expensive than oil.[39] She argues that water is a fundamental human right, not an economic commodity. She points out how changing our attitudes about water would be a herculean task, involving civil servants, activists, scholars, business leaders, religious leaders, governments, and communities. In other words, real change that would alleviate pollution and improve water access for the poor would require a complete and total change of the current system. It would indeed be a new thing.

Peppard also asks what theological traditions, either past or present, could "help us think through and articulate alternative frameworks of value and courses of action regarding global fresh water scarcity in the twenty-first century."[40] John's Apocalypse can be just one of these traditions. John grasps the connection between empire, economics, and environmental devastation. For him, this is an affront to creation. The vision of the New Jerusalem that John offers at the end of Revelation is one that finds no basis in the economic system of its day or in that of our day, for that matter. It seems rooted instead in an understanding of God as the creator and sustainer; God alone will provide food and water for all in the new city.[41]

39. Peppard, *Just Water*, 49.
40. Ibid., 51.
41. See Barbara R. Rossing, "River of Life in God's New Jerusalem: An Ecological Vision for the Earth's Future," *Mission Studies* 16 (1999): 136–56.

Peppard turns to the Vatican II document *Gaudium et Spes* to show that the goods of creation are meant for all people equally:

> The "universal destination of earthly goods" supersedes even legitimate, societal forms of property. This amounts to a radical statement of distributive justice: "everything contained in" the earth is intended by God "for the use of all human beings and peoples . . . for all in like manner."[42]

Our thirst slurps from the resources of those who are less fortunate. The economic lust of wealthy and powerful societies has created an environmental situation that puts us in the ecological debt of the poor. The way to pay off this debt is not to take small measures but to rethink the very structure of our economic system and our society. This should make us uncomfortable. One of my favorite bumper stickers says: "If you're not appalled, you're not paying attention." What the book of Revelation requires of us, when we read it ecologically, should appall us. Our discourse about how to save the environment today often falls to platitudes and things we do to make ourselves feel better. A three-minute segment on *Good Morning America* will not save the planet. When it comes to facing the deep structural challenges that our society puts on the planet, something totally new is needed.

V. Conclusion: Virtuosic Environmentalists

At the end of Revelation, an angel says to John: "Blessed is the one who keeps the words of the prophecy of this book" (Rev 22:7). In our ecological context, the words of this prophecy place a significant burden upon those who would seek to keep them. It would require life decisions that would puzzle your friends and family. It would require advocacy—for new policies, processes, or peoples—that agitate your government. John's audience faced persecution and, at times, death, for not capitulating to the empire of its day. While our empire today may not be as overtly religious, it still honors profit

---

42. Peppard, *Just Water*, 59. Peppard is quoting from *Gaudium et Spes* 69.

over people, selfishness over sharing, advancement over animals, and progress over the planet. In so doing, we make ourselves gods, whom we worship unflinchingly.

An apocalyptic ecology sees the world differently and follows God's lead in creating a new world. John's words become true when we use our collective imaginations to create the world that John envisions.[43] This does not mean we copy the destruction in Revelation, but that we imagine an alternative to the ways of empire, a world in which all of creation is nurtured and the economic system of destruction no longer exists. It is God's work, to be sure. But those who are blessed will "wash their robes" (Rev 22:14), which means they choose to live outside the empire and pay the price for it.

A new ecological future will require new creativity. John Ehrenfeld turns to artists as an example:

> The creative act of designing brings forth something from nothing. It is how artists, writers, and musicians show their virtuosity. . . . None of them bring their future visions into being by following their present GPS systems. They have all learned to make metaphorical jumps that allow them to transcend the limits of commonplace rationality. How they act is never "reasonable."[44]

Based on what we have explored in this book and how Revelation envisions the future, I cannot offer here a concrete list of action items. In the movie *Contact*, based on a book by Carl Sagan, the main character travels through a wormhole and is the first human in history to see up close a new part of the universe. As a scientist, she is speechless and says: "They should have sent a poet." Envisioning a new world cannot be left to the technocrats. We all need to think poetically, to be virtuosic environmentalists, in order to achieve a sustainable future.

The book of Revelation ends with an invitation for anyone who thirsts or hears to come and drink freely:

43. See Luke Timothy Johnson, "How Is the Bible True?" *Commonweal* (May 2009). Accessed online https://www.commonwealmagazine.org/how-bible-true-0.

44. Ehrenfeld, *Sustainability by Design*, 63.

The Spirit and the bride say, "Come."
And let everyone who hears say, "Come."
And let everyone who is thirsty come.
Let anyone who wishes take the water of life as a gift. (Rev 22:17)

This is a depiction of an utterly new reality. It is not an ecological manifesto, but an invitation to live differently that today we must give an ecological interpretation. The end of Revelation wants a new beginning. The end, it turns out, is just another place to start.

Bibliography

Aberth, John. *An Environmental History of the Middle Ages: The Crucible of Nature.* London: Routledge, 2013.

———. *From the Brink of the Apocalypse: Confronting Famine, War, Plague and Death in the Later Middle Ages.* London: Routledge, 2009.

Adams, Edward. *The Stars Will Fall from Heaven: "Cosmic Catastrophe" in the New Testament and Its World.* LNTS. London: T&T Clark, 2007.

Anson, Edward M. *Alexander's Heirs: The Age of the Successors.* Chichester: Wiley-Blackwell, 2014.

Apuleius. *The Golden Ass.* Translated by P. G. Walsh. Oxford: Oxford University Press, 1994.

Arbuckle, Benjamin. "Large Game Depression and the Process of Animal Domestication in the Near East." In *Climate and Ancient Societies,* edited by Susanne Kerner, Rachael J. Dann, and Pernille Bangsgaard, 215–44. Copenhagen: Museum Tusculanum Press, 2015.

Argall, Randal A. *1 Enoch and Sirach: A Comparative Literary and Conceptual Analysis of the Themes of Revelation, Creation and Judgment.* Atlanta: Scholars Press, 1995.

Arnell, Nigel W. "Climate Change and Global Water Resources." *Global Environmental Change* 9 (1999): 31–49.

Auguet, Roland. *Cruelty and Civilization: The Roman Games.* London: Allen and Unwin, 1972.

Aune, David E. *Revelation.* Word Biblical Commentary Series. 3 vols. Grand Rapids, MI: Zondervan, 1997.

Austin, Michael M. "Hellenistic Kings, War, and the Economy." *The Classical Quarterly* 36, no. 2 (1986): 450–66.

———. *The Hellenistic World from Alexander to the Roman Conquest: A Selection of Ancient Sources in Translation.* Cambridge: Cambridge University Press, 2006.

Baer, Hans A. *The Anthropology of Climate Change: An Integrated Critical Perspective.* London: Routledge, 2014.

Bagnall, Roger S., and Peter Derow, eds. *Greek Historical Documents: The Hellenistic Period*. Chico, CA: Scholars Press, 1981.

Baker, Alan. *The Gladiator: The Secret History of Rome's Warrior Slaves*. New York: St. Martin's Press, 2001.

Bakhos, Carol. *Ancient Judaism in Its Hellenistic Context*. Supplements to the Journal for the Study of Judaism Series. Leiden: Brill, 2005.

Barker, Margaret. *Creation: A Biblical Vision for the Environment*. London: T&T Clark, 2010.

Bar-Kochva, Bezalel. *The Seleucid Army: Organization and Tactics in the Great Campaigns*. Cambridge: Cambridge University Press, 2012.

Barnett, Paul. "Polemical Parallelism: Some Further Reflections on the Apocalypse." *Journal for the Study of the New Testament* 35 (1989): 111–20.

Barr, David L. *Tales of the End: A Narrative Commentary on the Book of Revelation*. Santa Rosa, CA: Polebridge Press, 1998.

Barton, Carlin A. *The Sorrows of the Ancient Romans: The Gladiator and the Monster*. Princeton, NJ: Princeton University Press, 1992.

Bauckham, Richard. *The Bible and Ecology: Rediscovering the Community of Creation*. Waco, TX: Baylor University Press, 2010.

———. *Climax of Prophecy: Studies on the Book of Revelation*. London: T&T Clark, 2000.

———. *Living with Other Creatures: Green Exegesis and Theology*. Waco, TX: Baylor University Press, 2011.

———. *The Theology of the Book of Revelation*. Cambridge: Cambridge University Press, 1993.

———. *Theology of Jürgen Moltmann*. London: T&T Clark, 1995.

Beard, Mary. *The Parthenon*. Cambridge, MA: Harvard University Press, 2003.

Benson, Robert G., and Susan J. Ridyard, eds. *Man and Nature in the Middle Ages*. Sewanee, TN: University of the South Press, 1995.

Bergant, Dianne. "Is the Biblical Worldview Anthropocentric?" *New Theology Review* 4 (1991): 5–14.

Berlin, Andrea M. "Between Large Forces: Palestine in the Hellenistic Period." *Biblical Archaeologist* 60, no. 1 (1997): 2–51.

Betlyon, John Wilson. "Archaeological Evidence of Military Operations in Southern Judah during the Early Hellenistic Period." *Biblical Archaeologist* 54, no. 1 (1991): 36–43.

Bigg, G. R., et al. "The Role of the Oceans in Climate." *International Journal of Climatology* 23, no. 10 (2003): 1127–1159.

Bilde, Per. *Aspects of Hellenistic Kingship*. Aarhus: Aarhus University Press, 1996.

Bilsky, Lester J. *Historical Ecology: Essays on Environment and Social Change.* Port Washington, NY: Kennikat Press, 1980.

Blount, Brian K. *Revelation: A Commentary.* The New Testament Library Series. Louisville, KY: Westminster John Knox Press, 2009.

Boatwright, Mary Taliaferro. "Theaters in the Roman Empire." *Biblical Archaeologist* 53, no. 4 (1990): 184–92.

Boff, Leonardo. *Cry of the Earth, Cry of the Poor.* Maryknoll, NY: Orbis Books, 1997.

Bolman, Elizabeth S. "De Coloribus: The Meanings of Color in Beatus Manuscripts." *Gesta* 38 (1999): 22–34.

Bottema, Sytze, and Henk Woldring. "Anthropogenic Indicators in the Pollen Record of the Eastern Mediterranean." In *Man's Role in the Shaping of the Eastern Mediterranean Landscape.* Edited by S. Bottema, G. Entjes-Nieborg, and W. van Zeist, 231–64. Rotterdam: A. A. Balkema, 1990.

Boxall, Ian. "The Apocalypse Unveiled: Reflections on the Reception History of Revelation." *The Expository Times* 125, no. 6 (2014): 261–71.

———. *Patmos in the Reception History of the Apocalypse.* Oxford: Oxford University Press, 2013.

Bratton, Susan. *Environmental Values in Christian Art.* Albany: State University of New York Press, 2008.

Breed, Brennan W. *Nomadic Text: A Theory of Biblical Reception History.* Bloomington: Indiana University Press, 2014.

Brieger, Peter H., and Marthe Dulong. *The Trinity College Apocalypse: An Introduction and Description by Peter H. Brieger.* London: Eugrammia Press, 1967.

Brueggemann, Walter. "Faith at the *Nullpunkt.*" In *The End of the World and the Ends of God*, edited by John Polkinghorne and Michael Welker, 143–54. Harrisburg, PA: Trinity Press International, 2000.

Bultmann, Rudolf. "Ist die Apokalyptik die Mutter der christlichen Theologie?" In *Apophoreta: Festschrift für Ernst Haenchen*, edited by Walther Eltester and Franz H. Kettler, 64–69. Berlin: Töpelmann, 1964.

Campbell, Brian, and Lawrence A. Tritle. *The Oxford Handbook of Warfare in the Classical World.* Oxford: Oxford University Press, 2013.

Carter, Michael J. D. "The Presentation of Gladiatorial Spectacles in the Greek East: Roman Culture and Greek Identity." PhD diss., McMaster University, 1999.

Chaniotis, Angelos. *War in the Hellenistic World: A Social and Cultural History.* Oxford: Wiley-Blackwell, 2008.

Charlesworth, James H., ed. *The Old Testament Pseudepigrapha.* Vol. 1, *Apocalyptic Literature and Testaments.* Garden City, NY: Doubleday, 1983.

Chilton, Bruce. *Visions of the Apocalypse: Receptions of John's Revelation in Western Imagination*. Waco, TX: Baylor University Press, 2013.

Clark, Willene. "Zoology in the Medieval Latin Bestiary." In *Man and Nature in the Middle Ages*, edited by Robert G. Benson and Susan J. Ridyard, 223–38. Sewanee, TN: University of the South Press, 1995.

Clason, Christopher. "'Gebrochen bluomen unde gras': Medieval Ecological Consciousness in Selected Poems by Walther von der Vogelweide." In *Rural Space in the Middle Ages and Early Modern Age: The Spatial Turn in Premodern Studies*, edited by Albrecht Classen, 227–50. Berlin: Walter de Gruyter, 2012.

Classen, Albrecht. "The Discovery of the Mountain as an Epistemological Challenge: A Paradigm Shift in the Approach to Highly Elevated Nature. Petrarch's *Ascent to Mont Ventoux* and Emperor Maximilian's *Theuerdank*." In *The Book of Nature and Humanity*, edited by David Hawkes and Richard G. Newhauser, 3–18. Turnhout: Brepols, 2013.

Clifford, Richard J. "The Roots of Apocalypticism in Near Eastern Myth." In *The Encyclopedia of Apocalypticism*. Vol. 1, *The Origins of Apocalypticism in Judaism and Christianity*, edited by John J. Collins, 3–38. New York: Continuum, 1998.

Collins, Adela Yarbro. *Crisis and Catharsis: The Power of the Apocalypse*. Philadelphia: Westminster Press, 1984.

———. *The Combat Myth in the Book of Revelation*. Missoula, MT: Scholars Press, 1976.

Collins, John J. *The Apocalyptic Imagination: An Introduction to Jewish Apocalyptic Literature*. Grand Rapids, MI: Eerdmans, 1998.

Concannon, Cavan W. "'Not for an Olive Wreath, but Our Lives': Gladiators, Athletes, and Early Christian Bodies." *Journal of Biblical Literature* 133 (2014): 193–214.

Cone, James H. *Martin & Malcolm & America: A Dream or a Nightmare?* Maryknoll, NY: Orbis Books, 2012.

Cronon, William. "The Trouble with Wilderness: Or, Getting Back to the Wrong Nature." *Environmental History* 1 (1996): 7–28.

Cuomo, Serafina. *Technology and Culture in Greek and Roman Antiquity*. Cambridge: Cambridge University Press, 2007.

Deckers, Jan. "Christianity and Ecological Ethics: The Significance of Process Thought and a Panexperientialist Critique of Strong Anthropocentrism." *Ecotheology: Journal of Religion, Nature and the Environment* 9, no. 3 (2004): 359–87.

Diodorus Siculus. *Library of History*. Translated by C. H. Oldfather. 11 vols. Loeb Classical Library. Cambridge, MA: Harvard University Press, 1935.

Donohoe, Martin. "Causes and Health Consequences of Environmental Degradation and Social Injustice." *Social Science & Medicine* 56, no. 3 (2003): 573–87.

Ehrenfeld, John R. *Sustainability by Design: A Subversive Strategy for Transforming Our Consumer Culture.* New Haven, CT: Yale University Press, 2009.

――― and Andrew J. Hoffman. *Flourishing: A Frank Conversation about Sustainability.* Stanford, CA: Stanford Business Books, 2013.

Emmerson, Richard Kenneth, and Bernard McGinn. *The Apocalypse in the Middle Ages.* Ithaca, NY: Cornell University Press, 1992.

Epplett, William Christopher. "Animal Spectacula of the Roman Empire." PhD diss., University of British Columbia, 2001.

Fagan, Garrett G. *The Lure of the Arena: Social Psychology and the Crowd at the Roman Games.* Cambridge: Cambridge University Press, 2011.

Fiorenza, Elisabeth Schüssler. *Revelation: Vision of a Just World.* Minneapolis: Fortress Press, 1991.

Fretheim, Terence E. *God and World in the Old Testament: A Relational Theology of Creation.* Nashville, TN: Abingdon Press, 2010.

Friesen, Steven J. "The Cult of the Roman Emperors in Ephesos: Temple Wardens, City Titles, and the Interpretation of the Revelation of John." In *Ephesos: Metropolis of Asia: An Interdisciplinary Approach to its Archaeology, Religion, and Culture,* edited by Helmut Koester, 229–50. Valley Forge, PA: Trinity Press International, 1995.

―――. *Imperial Cults and the Apocalypse of John: Reading Revelation in the Ruins.* Oxford: Oxford University Press, 2001.

―――. "Revelation, Realia, and Religion: Archaeology in the Interpretation of the Apocalypse." *Harvard Theological Review* 88, no. 3 (1995): 291–314.

―――. *Twice Neokoros: Ephesus, Asia, and the Cult of the Flavian Imperial Family.* Leiden: Brill, 1993.

Frilingos, Christopher. *Spectacles of Empire: Monsters, Martyrs, and the Book of Revelation.* Philadelphia: University of Pennsylvania Press, 2004.

Fromm, Erich. *To Have or To Be?* Reprint edition. London: Bloomsbury Academic, 2013.

Futrell, Alison. *Blood in the Arena: The Spectacle of Roman Power.* Austin, TX: University of Texas Press, 1997.

―――. *The Roman Games: A Sourcebook.* Malden, MA: Blackwell Publishing, 2006.

Galbraith, John Kenneth. "How Much Should a Country Consume?" In *Perspectives on Conservation: Essays on America's Natural Resources,* edited by Henry Jarrett. Baltimore: Johns Hopkins University Press, 1958.

Gilbertson, Michael. *God and History in the Book of Revelation: New Testament Studies in Dialogue with Pannenberg and Moltmann*. Cambridge: Cambridge University Press, 2005.

Gilhus, Ingvild Saelid. *Animals, Gods, and Humans: Changing Attitudes to Animals in Greek, Roman, and Early Christian Thought*. London: Routledge, 2006.

Gornitz, Vivien, Stephen Couch, and Ellen Hartig. "Impacts of Sea Level Rise in the New York City Metropolitan Area." *Global and Planetary Change* 32, no. 1 (2001): 61–88.

Grainger, John D. *The Syrian Wars*. Leiden: Brill, 2010.

Green, Peter. *Alexander to Actium: The Historical Evolution of the Hellenistic Age*. Berkeley: University of California Press, 1993.

Grossman, Michael Orlov, and Ronald Eric Matthews, Jr. *Perspectives on the Legacy of George W. Bush*. Newcastle upon Tyne: Cambridge Scholars Publishing, 2008.

Guha, Ramachandra. "Radical American Environmentalism and Wilderness Preservation: A Third World Critique." *Environmental Ethics* 11, no. 1 (1989): 71–83.

Gunderson, Erik. "The Ideology of the Arena." *Classical Antiquity* 15, no. 1 (1996): 113–51.

Habel, Norman C., ed. *Readings from the Perspective of Earth*. Sheffield: Sheffield Academic Press, 2000.

——— and Vicky Balabanski, eds. *The Earth Story in the New Testament*. London: Sheffield Academic Press, 2002.

——— and Peter L. Trudinger, eds. *Exploring Ecological Hermeneutics*. Atlanta: Society of Biblical Literature, 2008.

Hallman, David G., ed. *Ecotheology: Voices from South and North*. Maryknoll, NY: Orbis Books, 1994.

Harnischfeger, Ernst. *Die Bamberger Apokalypse*. Stuttgart: Urachhaus, 1981.

Hassall, A. G., and W. O. Hassall. *The Douce Apocalypse*. New York: T. Yoseloff, 1961.

Hawkin, David J. "The Critique of Ideology in the Book of Revelation and Its Implications for Ecology." *Ecotheology* 8, no. 2 (2003): 161–72.

Hays, Richard B., and Stefan Alkier, eds. *Revelation and the Politics of Apocalyptic Interpretation*. Waco, TX: Baylor University Press, 2015.

Healy, John F. *Mining and Metallurgy in the Greek and Roman World*. London: Thames and Hudson, 1978.

Heck, Christian, and Rémy Cordonnier. *The Grand Medieval Bestiary: Animals in Illuminated Manuscripts*. New York: Abbeville Press, 2012.

Hessel, Dieter T. *Theology for Earth Community: A Field Guide.* Maryknoll, NY: Orbis Books, 1996.

——— and Rosemary Radford Ruether, eds. *Christianity and Ecology: Seeking the Well-Being of Earth and Humans.* Cambridge, MA: Harvard University Press, 2000.

Hirt, Alfred Michael. *Imperial Mines and Quarries in the Roman World: Organizational Aspects 27 BC–AD 235.* Oxford: Oxford University Press, 2010.

Hodder, Ian. *Entangled: An Archaeology of the Relationships between Humans and Things.* Malden, MA: Wiley-Blackwell, 2012.

Hoegh-Guldberg, O., P. J. Mumby, A. J. Hotten, R. S. Steneck, P. Greenfield, E. Gomez, and C. D. Harvell. "Coral Reefs Under Rapid Climate Change and Ocean Acidification." *Science* 318, no. 5857 (2007): 1737–1742.

Hoffmann, Richard. *An Environmental History of Medieval Europe.* Cambridge: Cambridge University Press, 2014.

Hoover, Oliver. *Coins of the Seleucid Empire in the Collection of Arthur Houghton,* vol. 2. New York: American Numismatic Society, 2007.

Hornik, Heidi J., and Mikeal C. Parsons, eds. *Interpreting Christian Art: Reflections on Christian Art.* Macon, GA: Mercer University Press, 2003.

Horrell, David. *Bible and the Environment: Towards a Critical Ecological Biblical Theology.* London: Equinox Publishing, 2010.

Horrell, David, Cherryl Hunt, Christopher Southgate, and Francesca Stavrakopolou, eds. *Ecological Hermeneutics: Biblical, Historical and Theological Perspectives.* London: T&T Clark, 2010.

Houghton, Arthur, and Catherine Lorber, eds. *Seleucid Coins, A Comprehensive Catalog. Part 1: Seleucus I–Antiochus III.* Lancaster, PA: American Numismatic Society, 2003.

Huber, Lynn R. *Thinking and Seeing with Women in Revelation.* London: T&T Clark, 2013.

Hughes, Donald J. "Artemis: Goddess of Conservation." *Forest and Conservation History* 34, no. 4 (1990): 191–97.

———. *Environmental Problems of the Greeks and Romans: Ecology in the Ancient Mediterranean.* Baltimore: Johns Hopkins University Press, 2014.

———. "Warfare and Environment in the Ancient World." In *Oxford Handbook of Warfare in the Classical World*, edited by Brian Campbell and Lawrence A. Tritle, 128–42. Oxford: Oxford University Press, 2013.

Humphrey, John William, John Peter Oleson, and Andrew N. Sherwood. *Greek and Roman Technology: A Sourcebook.* London: Routledge, 2003.

Janik, Vincent M., and Paul M. Thompson. "Changes in Surfacing Patterns of Bottlenose Dolphins in Response to Boat Traffic." *Marine Mammal Science* 12, no. 4 (1996): 597–602.

Johns, Loren L. *The Lamb Christology of the Apocalypse of John: An Investigation into Its Origins and Rhetorical Force.* Wissenschaftliche Untersuchungen zum Neuen Testament. Tübingen: Mohr Siebeck, 2003.

Johnson, Luke Timothy. "How Is the Bible True?" *Commonweal.* May 18, 2009.

Jorgenson, Andrew K. "Consumption and Environmental Degradation: A Cross-national Analysis of the Ecological Footprint." *Social Problems* 50, no. 3 (2003): 374–94.

Josephus. *Jewish Antiquities 12–13.* 9 vols. Translated by H. St. J. Thackeray and Ralph Marcus. Loeb Classical Library. Cambridge, MA: Harvard University Press, 1943.

Kahan, Dan M., Ellen Peters, Maggie Wittlin, Paul Slovic, Lisa Larrimore Ouelette, Donald Braman, and Gregory Mandel. "The Polarizing Impact of Science Literacy and Numeracy on Perceived Climate Change Risks." *Nature Climate Change* 2, no. 10 (2012): 732–35.

Keller, Catherine. *Apocalypse Now and Then: A Feminist Guide to the End of the World.* Boston: Beacon Press, 1996.

Kerner, Susanne, Rachael J. Dann, and Pernille Bangsgaard. *Climate and Ancient Societies.* Copenhagen: Museum Tusculanum Press, 2015.

Klauck, Hans-Josef. "Do They Never Come Back? Nero Redivivus and the Apocalypse of John." *Catholic Biblical Quarterly* 63, no. 4 (2001): 683–98.

Klein, Peter K., ed. *Apokalypse, Ms. Douce 180: vollständige Faksimile-Ausgabe im Originalformat der Handschrift Ms. Douce 180 aus dem Besitz der Bodleian Library, Oxford.* Graz: Akademische Druck- u. Verlagsanstalt, 1983.

Klingender, F. D. *Animals in Art and Thought: To the End of the Middle Ages.* London: Routledge, 1971.

Koester, Craig R. *Revelation: A New Translation with Introduction and Commentary.* Edited by John J. Collins. Anchor Bible Series. New Haven, CT: Yale University Press, 2014.

Koester, Helmut, ed. *Ephesos Metropolis of Asia: An Interdisciplinary Approach to Its Archaeology, Religion, and Culture.* Cambridge, MA: Harvard University Press, 2004.

Kondoleon, Christine, and Bettina Ann Bergmann. *The Art of Ancient Spectacle.* Washington, DC: National Gallery of Art, 1999.

Kosmin, Paul J. *The Land of the Elephant Kings: Space, Territory, and Ideology in the Seleucid Empire.* Cambridge, MA: Harvard University Press, 2014.

Kovacs, Judith, and Christopher Rowland. *Revelation*. Blackwell Bible Commentaries. Oxford: Blackwell, 2004.

Kraybill, J. Nelson. *Apocalypse and Allegiance: Worship, Politics, and Devotion in the Book of Revelation*. Grand Rapids, MI: Brazos Press, 2010.

Kuhrt, Amélie, and Susan M. Sherwin-White, eds. *Hellenism in the East: The Interaction of Greek and Non-Greek Civilizations from Syria to Central Asia after Alexander*. Berkeley: University of California Press, 1987.

Kyle, Donald G. "Animal Spectacles in Ancient Rome: Meat and Meaning." In *Sport in the Greek and Roman Worlds*. Vol. 2: *Greek Athletic Identities and Roman Sports and Spectacle*, edited by Thomas F. Scanlon, 269–95. Oxford: Oxford University Press, 2014.

———. *Spectacles of Death in Ancient Rome*. London: Routledge, 1998.

Landau, Y. H. "A Greek Inscription Found Near Hefzibah." *Israel Exploration Journal* 16, no. 1 (1966): 54–70.

Landes, Richard Allen, Andrew Colin Gow, and David C. Van Meter, eds. *The Apocalyptic Year 1000: Religious Expectation and Social Change, 950–1050*. Oxford: Oxford University Press, 2003.

Laufner, Richard, and Peter K. Klein. *Trierer Apokalypse: vollständige Faksimile-Ausg. im Originalformat des Codex 31 der Stadtbibliothek Trier*. Graz: Akademische Druck- und Verlagsanstalt, 1974.

Leopold, Aldo. *A Sand County Almanac*. Reprint edition. New York: Ballantine Books, 1970.

Levine, Amy-Jill, and Maria Mayo Robbins, eds. *A Feminist Companion to the Apocalypse of John*. London: T&T Clark, 2010.

Lewis, Suzanne. *Reading Images: Narrative Discourse and Reception in the Thirteenth-Century Illuminated Apocalypse*. Cambridge: Cambridge University Press, 1995.

Licht, Lewis A., and John T. Ramsey. *The Comet of 44 B.C. and Caesar's Funeral Games*. Atlanta: Scholars Press, 1997.

LiDonnici, Lynn R. "The Images of Artemis Ephesia and Greco-Roman Worship: A Reconsideration." *Harvard Theological Review* 85, no. 4 (1992): 389–415.

Lipschitz, Oded, Gary N. Knoppers, and Rainer Albertz. *Judah and the Judaeans in the Fourth Century B.C.E.* Winona Lake, IN: Eisenbrauns, 2007.

Long, Matthew C., Curtis Deutsch, and Ito Taka. "Finding Forced Trends in Oceanic Oxygen: Trends in Dissolved Oxygen." *Global Biogeochemical Cycles* 30, no. 2 (2016): 381–97.

Longcore, Travis, and Catherine Rich. "Ecological Light Pollution." *Frontiers in Ecology and the Environment* 2, no. 4 (2004): 191–98.

Love, Glen A. *Practical Ecocriticsm: Literature, Biology, and the Environment*. Charlottesville: University of Virginia Press, 2003.

Lyons, William John, and Jorunn Kland, eds. *The Way the World Ends? The Apocalypse of John in Culture and Ideology*. Sheffield: Sheffield Phoenix Press, 2009.

MacMullen, Ramsay. *Enemies of the Roman Order: Treason, Unrest, and Alienation in the Empire*. Cambridge, MA: Harvard University Press, 1966.

Marsden, E. W. "Macedonian Military Machinery and Its Designers under Philip and Alexander." In *Ancient Macedonia II: Papers Read at the Second International Symposium held in Thessaloniki*, 211–23. Thessaloniki: Institute for Balkan Studies, 1977.

Martial. *Epigrams, Spectacles*. Books 1–5. Translated by D. R. Shackleton Bailey. Cambridge, MA: Harvard University Press, 1993.

Mattingly, D. J. *Imperialism, Power and Identity: Experiencing the Roman Empire*. Princeton, NJ: Princeton University Press, 2011.

Mayor, Adrienne. *Greek Fire, Poison Arrows, and Scorpion Bombs: Biological and Chemical Warfare in the Ancient World*. Woodstock, NY: Overlook Duckworth, 2003.

McGinn, Bernard. *Visions of the End: Apocalyptic Traditions in the Middle Ages*. New York: Columbia University Press, 1979.

McKitterick, David, ed. *The Trinity Apocalypse (Trinity College Cambridge, MS R.16.2)*. London: British Library, 2005.

Meiggs, Russell. *Trees and Timber in the Ancient Mediterranean World*. Oxford: Clarendon Press, 1982.

Mendelsohn, Robert, Ariel Dinar, and Larry Williams. "The Distributional Impact of Climate Change on Rich and Poor Countries." *Environment and Development Economics* 2 (2006): 159–78.

Middleton, Paul. *Radical Martyrdom and Cosmic Conflict in Early Christianity*. London: T&T Clark, 2006.

Miller, Richard W. *God, Creation, and Climate Change: A Catholic Response to the Environmental Crisis*. Maryknoll, NY: Orbis Books, 2010.

Mitchell, Stephen. *Anatolia: Land, Men, and Gods in Asia Minor*. Oxford: Clarendon Press, 1993.

Moe-Lobeda, Cynthia. *Resisting Structural Evil: Love as Ecological-Economic Vocation*. Minneapolis: Fortress Press, 2013.

Moleiro, Manuel, et al. *Códice de Santo Domingo de Silos*. Barcelona: M. Moleiro, 2001.

Moo, Douglas J. "Nature in the New Creation: New Testament Eschatology and the Environment." *Journal of the Evangelical Theological Society* 49, no. 3 (2006): 449–88.

Moo, Jonathan. "The Sea That Is No More: Rev 21:1 and the Function of Sea Imagery in the Apocalypse of John." *Novum Testamentum* 51, no. 2 (2009): 148–67.

Moore, Stephen D. *Untold Tales from the Book of Revelation: Sex and Gender, Empire and Ecology.* Atlanta: Society of Biblical Literature Press, 2014.

Morgan, Nigel J. *The Douce Apocalypse: Picturing the End of the World in the Middle Ages.* Oxford: Bodleian Library, 2006.

———. *Illuminating the End of Time: The Getty Apocalypse Manuscript.* Los Angeles: J. Paul Getty Museum, 2011.

Morton, John F. "The Impact of Climate Change on Smallholder and Subsistence Agriculture." *Proceedings of the National Academy of Sciences* 104, no. 50 (2007): 19680–19685.

Murphy-O'Connor, Jerome. *St. Paul's Ephesus: Texts and Archaeology.* Collegeville, MN: Liturgical Press, 2008.

Naess, Arne. "The Basics of Deep Ecology." *Trumpeter* 21, no. 1 (2005): 61–71.

———. "The Shallow and the Deep: Long-range Ecology Movement, A Summary." *Inquiry* 16 (1973): 95–100.

Navara, Kristen J., and Randy J. Nelson. "The Dark Side of Night: Physiological, Epidemiological, and Ecological Consequences." *Journal of Pineal Research* 43, no. 3 (2007): 215–24.

Neef, Reinder. "Introduction, Development and Environmental Implications of Olive Culture: The Evidence from Jordan." In *Man's Role in the Shaping of the Eastern Mediterranean Landscape,* edited by S. Bottema, G. Entjes-Nieborg, and W. van Zeist, 295–306. Rotterdam: A. A. Balkema, 1990.

Nickelsburg, George W. E. *1 Enoch: A Commentary on the Book of 1 Enoch Chapters 1–36.* Hermeneia Series. Minneapolis: Fortress Press, 2001.

——— and VanderKam, James C. *1 Enoch: A New Translation Based on the Hermeneia Commentary.* Minneapolis: Fortress Press, 2004.

Nicolet, Claude. *Space, Geography, and Politics in the Early Roman Empire.* Ann Arbor: University of Michigan Press, 1991.

Northcott, Michael. "Girard, Climate Change, and Apocalypse." In *Can We Survive Our Origins? Readings in René Girard's Theory of Violence and the Sacred,* edited by Pierpaolo Antonello and Paul Gifford, 287–309. East Lansing: Michigan State University Press, 2015.

O'Brien, Karen L. and Robin M. Leichenko. "Double Exposure: Assessing the Impacts of Climate Change within the Context of Economic Globalization." *Global Environmental Change* 10, no. 3 (2000): 221–32.

O'Hear, Natasha. *Contrasting Images of the Book of Revelation in Late Medieval and Early Modern Art: A Case Study in Visual Exegesis.* Oxford: Oxford University Press, 2011.

——— and Anthony O'Hear. *Picturing the Apocalypse: The Book of Revelation in the Arts over Two Millennia.* Oxford: Oxford University Press, 2015.

O'Kane, Martin. *Painting the Text: The Artist as Biblical Interpreter*. Sheffield: Sheffield Phoenix Press, 2007.

Oleson, John Peter. *The Oxford Handbook of Engineering and Technology in the Classical World*. Oxford: Oxford University Press, 2008.

Orr, David W. "Armageddon versus Extinction." *Conservation Biology* 19, no. 2 (2005): 290–92.

Oster, Richard. "Christianity and Emperor Veneration in Ephesus: Iconography of a Conflict." *Restoration Quarterly* 25, no. 3 (1982): 143–49.

———. *Ephesus as a Religious Center under the Principate, I: Paganism before Constantine*. Berlin: Walter de Gruyter, 1990.

Palmer, James T. *The Apocalypse in the Middle Ages*. Cambridge: Cambridge University Press, 2014.

Patella, Michael. *Word and Image: The Hermeneutics of the Saint John's Bible*. Collegeville, MN: Liturgical Press, 2013.

Peppard, Christiana Z. *Just Water: Theology, Ethics, and the Global Water Crisis*. Maryknoll, NY: Orbis Books, 2014.

Pimm, S. L. "The Biodiversity of Species and Their Rates of Extinction, Distribution, and Protection. *Science* 344 (2014): 1246752-1– 1246752-10.

Pippin, Tina. *Apocalyptic Bodies and the Biblical End of the World in Text and Image*. London: Routledge, 1999.

———. *Death and Desire: The Rhetoric of Gender in the Apocalypse of John*. Louisville, KY: Westminster John Knox Press, 1992.

Plato. *Timaeus, Critias, Cleitophon, Menexenus, Epistles*. Translated by R. G. Bury. Loeb Classical Library. Cambridge, MA: Harvard University Press, 1929.

Pliny the Elder. *Natural History*. 10 vols. Loeb Classical Library. Translated by H. Rackham. Cambridge, MA: Harvard University Press, 1952.

Plutarch. *Lives: Agis and Cleomenes, Tiberius and Gaius Gracchus, Philopoemen and Famininus*. Translated by Bernadotte Perrin. Loeb Classical Library. Cambridge, MA: Harvard University Press, 1921.

———. *Lives: Agesilaus and Pompey, Pelopidas and Marcellus*. Translated by Bernadotte Perrin. Loeb Classical Library. Cambridge, MA: Harvard University Press, 1917.

Polkinghorne, John, and Michael Welker, eds. *The End of the World and the Ends of God: Science and Theology on Eschatology*. Harrisburg, PA: Trinity Press International, 2000.

Pollard, Nigel. *Soldiers, Cities, and Civilians in Roman Syria*. Ann Arbor: University of Michigan Press, 2000.

Polybius. *The Histories.* 6 vols. Translated by W. R. Paton. Loeb Classical Library. Cambridge, MA: Harvard University Press, 1923.

Ponting, Clive. *A Green History of the World: The Environment and the Collapse of Great Civilizations.* New York: Penguin Books, 1991.

Portier-Young, Anathea. *Apocalypse against Empire: Theologies of Resistance in Early Judaism.* Grand Rapids, MI: Eerdmans, 2011.

Potamianos, Christos. "The Function of the Roman Spectacle in Ephesos." MA thesis, University of California, Santa Barbara, 2011.

Potts, Simon G., Jacobus C. Biesmeijer, Claire Kremen, Peter Neumann, Oliver Schweiger, and William E. Kunin. "Global Pollinator Declines: Trends, Impacts and Drivers." *Trends in Ecology and Evolution* 25, no. 6 (2010): 345–53.

Price, S. R. F. *Rituals and Power: The Roman Imperial Cult in Asia Minor.* Cambridge: Cambridge University Press, 1984.

Redman, Charles L. *The Archaeology of Global Change: The Impact of Humans on their Environment.* Washington, DC: Smithsonian Books, 2004.

———. *Human Impact on Ancient Environments.* Tucson: University of Arizona Press, 1999.

Rhoads, David, ed. *From Every People and Nation.* Minneapolis: Fortress Press, 2005.

Richard, Pablo. *Apocalypse: A People's Commentary on the Book of Revelation.* Maryknoll, NY: Orbis Books, 1995.

Rogers, Guy MacLean. *The Mysteries of Artemis of Ephesos: Cult, Polis, and Change in the Graeco-Roman World.* New Haven, CT: Yale University Press, 2012.

Rossing, Barbara R. "Alas for the Earth! Lament and Resistance in Revelation 12." In *The Earth Story in the New Testament,* edited by Norman C. Habel and Vicky Balabanski, 180–92. London: Sheffield Academic Press, 2002.

———. *The Choice Between Two Cities: Whore, Bride, and Empire in the Apocalypse.* Harrisburg, PA: Trinity Press International, 1999.

———. "For the Healing of the World: Reading Revelation Ecologically." In *From Every People and Nation: The Book of Revelation in Intercultural Perspective,* edited by David Rhoads, 165–82. Minneapolis: Fortress Press, 2005.

———. *The Rapture Exposed: The Message of Hope in the Book of Revelation.* New York: Basic Books, 2004.

———. "River of Life in God's New Jerusalem: An Ecological Vision for Earth's Future." *Mission Studies* 16 (1999): 136–56.

Rubenstein, Mary-Jane. *Worlds without End: The Many Lives of the Multiverse.* New York: Columbia University Press, 2014.

Russell, David M. *The "New Heavens and New Earth": Hope for the Creation in Jewish Apocalyptic and the New Testament.* Philadelphia: Visionary Press, 1996.

Sabin, Philip, Hans van Wees, and Michael Whitby, eds. *The Cambridge History of Greek and Roman Warfare.* Cambridge: Cambridge University Press, 2007.

Sacchi, Paulo. *Jewish Apocalyptic and its History.* Translated by W. Short. Journal for the Study of Judaism Supplement Series. Sheffield: JSOT Press, 1990.

Sage, Michael M. *Warfare in Ancient Greece: A Sourcebook.* London: Routledge, 1996.

Salisbury, Joyce E. *The Beast Within: Animals in the Middle Ages.* London: Routledge, 1994.

Sallares, Robert. *The Ecology of the Ancient Greek World.* Ithaca, NY: Cornell University Press, 1991.

Sánchez, David A. *From Patmos to the Barrio: Subverting Imperial Myths.* Minneapolis: Fortress Press, 2008.

Scarborough, Connie, ed. *Fundamentals of Medieval and Early Modern Culture.* Vol. 13: *Inscribing the Environment: Ecocritical Approaches to Medieval Spanish Literature.* Hawthorne, NY, and Berlin: Walter de Gruyter, 2013.

Schmid, H. H. "Creation, Righteousness, and Salvation: 'Creation Theology' as the Broad Horizon of Biblical Theology." In *Old Testament Theology,* edited by Bernhard W. Anderson, 102–17. Minneapolis: Fortress Press, 1985.

Sears, Elizabeth, Thelma K. Thomas, and Ilene H. Forsyth, eds. *Reading Medieval Images: The Art Historian and the Object.* Ann Arbor: University of Michigan Press, 2002.

Serrati, John. "The Hellenistic World at War: Stagnation or Development?" In *Oxford Handbook of Warfare in the Classical World,* edited by Brian Campbell and Lawrence A. Tritle, 179–98. Oxford: Oxford University Press, 2013.

Shelton, Jo-Ann. *As the Romans Did: A Source Book in Roman Social History.* Oxford: Oxford University Press, 1988.

Sherwin-White, Susan, and Amélie Kuhrt, eds. *From Samarkhand to Sardis: A New Approach to the Seleucid Empire.* Berkeley: University of California Press, 1993.

Shipley, Graham. *The Greek World after Alexander, 323–30 B.C.* London: Routledge, 2000.

Siewers, Alfred K. *Strange Beauty: Ecocritical Approaches to Early Medieval Landscape.* New York: Palgrave Macmillan, 2009.

Simkins, Ronald A., and John J. O'Keefe. "The Greening of the Papacy." *Journal of Religion and Society Supplement Series* 9 (2013): 5–15.

Smith, R. R. R. "The Imperial Reliefs from the Sebasteion at Aphrodisias." *The Journal of Roman Studies* 77 (1987): 88–138.

Snyder, James. "The Reconstruction of an Early Christian Cycle of Illustrations for the Book of Revelation: The Trier Apocalypse." *Vigilae Christianae* 18, no. 3 (1964): 146–62.

Southgate, Christopher. *The Groaning of Creation: God, Evolution, and the Problem of Evil.* Louisville, KY: Westminster John Knox Press, 2008.

Stanbury, Sarah. "Ecochaucer: Green Ethics and Medieval Nature." *The Chaucer Review* 39, no. 1 (2004): 1–16.

Steinhauser, Kenneth B. "Narrative and Illumination in the Beatus Apocalypse." *The Catholic Historical Review* 81, no. 2 (1995): 185–210.

Stephens, Mark B. *Annihilation or Renewal? The Meaning and Function of New Creation in the Book of Revelation.* Wissenschaftliche Untersuchungen zum Neuen Testament. Tübingen: Mohr Siebeck, 2011.

Stone, Michael E. "The Parabolic Use of Natural Order in Judaism of the Second Temple Age." In *Gilgul: Essays on Transformation, Revolution, and Permanence in the History of Religions, Dedicated to R. J. Zwi Werblowsky,* edited by S. Shaked, D. Shulman, and G. G. Stroumsa, 298–308. Leiden: Brill, 1987.

Stuckenbruck, Loren T. "The Origins of Evil in Jewish Apocalyptic Tradition: The Interpretation of Genesis 6:1-4 in the Second and Third Centuries BCE." In *The Fall of the Angels,* edited by Christoph Auffarth and Loren T. Stuckenbruck, 87–118. Leiden: Brill, 2004.

Tanner, Kathryn. "Eschatology without a Future?" In *The End of the World and the Ends of God,* edited by John Polkinghorne and Michael Welker, 222–37. Harrisburg, PA: Trinity Press International, 2000.

———. *God and Creation in Christian Theology.* Minneapolis: Augsburg Fortress Press, 2004.

Tcherikover, Victor. *Hellenistic Civilization and the Jews.* New York: Macmillan, 2001.

Tertullian. *Apology, De Spectaculis.* Translated by T. R. Glover and Gerald H. Rendall. Loeb Classical Library. Cambridge, MA: Harvard University Press, 1931.

Theophrastus. *De Causis Plantarum.* 3 volumes. Loeb Classical Library. Translated by Arthur Hort. Cambridge, MA: Harvard University Press, 1916.

Thommen, Lukas. *An Environmental History of Ancient Greece and Rome.* Cambridge: Cambridge University Press, 2012.

Thorne, James A. "Warfare and Agriculture: The Economic Impact of Devastation in Classical Greece." *Greek, Roman and Byzantine Studies* 42, no. 3 (2001): 225–53.

Tilley, Christopher Y. *Interpreting Landscapes: Geologies, Topographies, Identities.* Walnut Creek, CA: Left Coast Press, 2009.

Trebilco, Paul R. *The Early Christians in Ephesus from Paul to Ignatius.* Tübingen: Mohr Siebeck, 2004.

Van den Brom, L. J. "The Art of a 'Theo-Ecological' Interpretation." *Nederlands Theologisch Tijdschrift* 51, no. 4 (1997): 298–314.

Verbeke, Werner, Daniel Verhelst, and Andries Welkenhuysen, eds. *The Use and Abuse of Eschatology in the Middle Ages.* Leuven: Leuven University Press, 1988.

Visser, Derk. *Apocalypse as Utopian Expectation (800–1500): The Apocalypse Commentary of Berengaudus of Ferrières and the Relationship between Exegesis, Liturgy, and Iconography.* Leiden: Brill, 1996.

Walker, B. H., and David Salt. *Resilience Thinking: Sustaining Ecosystems and People in a Changing World.* Washington, DC: Island Press, 2006.

Welch, Katherine. "Negotiating Roman Spectacle Architecture in the Greek World: Athens and Corinth." In *The Art of Ancient Spectacle*, edited by Bettina Ann Bergmann and Christine Kondoleon, 125–46. Washington, DC: National Gallery of Art, 1999.

White, Lynn, Jr. "The Historical Roots of Our Ecological Crisis." *Science* 155 (1967): 1203–1207.

Whittaker Hunter, Leslie, and S. A. Handford. *Aineiou Poliorketika.* Oxford: Clarendon Press, 1927.

Wiedemann, Thomas. *Emperors and Gladiators.* London: Routledge, 1992.

Williams, John. *The Illustrated Beatus: A Corpus of Illustrations of the Commentary on the Apocalypse.* London: Harvey Miller Publishers, 1994.

Williams, John, and Barbara A. Shailor, eds. *A Spanish Apocalypse: The Morgan Beatus Manuscript.* New York: George Braziller and Pierpont Morgan Library, 1991.

Williamson, Tom. *Environment, Society and Landscape in Early Medieval England: Time and Topography.* Woodbridge, UK: Boydell and Brewer, 2012.

Yapp, W. B. *Birds in Medieval Manuscripts.* London: British Library, 1981.

Zanker, Paul. *The Power of Images in the Age of Augustus.* Ann Arbor: University of Michigan Press, 1990.

Subject and Author Index

Scripture Index